GOING WITH THE FLOW

NAVIGATING THE STREAMS OF LIFE

LINDA ESTES

Energion Publications
Gonzalez, FL
2018

Many blessings!

&, Linda

Scripture quotations taken from the New American Standard
Bible® (NASB), Copyright © 1960, 1962, 1963, 1968, 1971,
1972, 1973, 1975, 1977, 1995 by The Lockman Foundation
Used by permission. www.Lockman.org.

e-books:
Kindle: 978-1-63199-493-7
Adobe Digital Editions: 978-1-63199-492-0
iBooks: 978-1-63199-494-4
Google Play: 978-1-63199-495-1

Print:
ISBN10: 1-63199-491-3
ISBN13: 978-1-63199-491-3
Library of Congress Control Number: 2018930614

Energion Publications
P. O. Box 841
Gonzalez, FL 32560
850-525-3916

energion.com
pubs@energion.com

AND SO THE JOURNEY CONTINUES...

As I write the forward to this, my second devotional, my sweet husband, Alan, has been in Heaven for over a year now. It's mind boggling that I have already lived this long without him, eighteen months to be exact. There are days that I still think I hear him coming through the door. No, I'm not losing my mind. Others that have lost a spouse tell me that's normal. The time I have spent without him has been hard but not nearly as hard as it would be if I didn't know the Lord, and if I didn't have friends and family supporting me. Jesus has been my rock and He has abundantly blessed me by putting so many beautiful people in my life.

As you read through these devotions, you will hear all about my Lord and Savior and how He has helped me day by day live a life that is pleasing to Him. Just like my first devotional, Alan will be found throughout these pages, too. Even though he is physically gone, I still carry Him in my heart and I'm looking forward to the day when I will join him and other loved ones that have entered Heaven before me.

God always knows what we need. For me, God knew I needed to stay knee deep in His Word to survive the loss of Alan, and so He gave me this project. Until the Lord takes me home, I will continue to do the Kingdom work He has given me. For now, my mission field is wherever this collection of devotions ends up. I appreciate you allowing me to share with you the things that the Lord is daily showing me. He is navigating the streams of my life and He will guide you through your life, too, if you let Him. My prayer is you will do just that.

1...THE ART OF RELAXATION

Good morning! The cover of this book was taken at Bennett Springs State Park in Missouri, my new favorite place to "unplug." Relaxation is becoming a lost art in this fast-paced world we live in. For most people, we don't have time to relax, as we have too much to do, and not enough hours in a day to get them done.

In the sixth chapter of Mark, I was reading about the disciples and their mission that God had given them. The mission trip put lots of demands on the disciples and when they returned from it, they were totally worn out, in every aspect of their lives ... physically, emotionally and spiritually.

I was struck by Jesus' response to their fatigue. No, Jesus didn't tell them to suck it up and deal with it, as we are often told in this world when we're just spent. His response came in verse 31. He said, "Come away by yourselves to a lonely place and rest for a while." I think I just heard a collective "YES" from all of us who have just been so tired that it's a struggle to get through the day.

If Jesus told His disciples to get away from everyone and rest, then it's safe to say that He is telling us the same thing. So when was the last time that you "unplugged" and got away from the daily demands of this world? From my experience, taking a few days of true R&R, and spending time communing with the Lord can make all the difference in your world. Praying you schedule some relaxation time in your busy life.

2...Lifelong Learners

Good morning! As a former teacher, one of the things I tried to instill in my students was the love of learning something new. I wanted to help them become a lifelong learner. I told them that at the point in their life where they didn't want to learn anything new, would be the point where they would really quit living.

The same principle is true in our Christian walk. We should want to learn something new about God every single day. 2 Timothy 3:16-17 tells us that, "All Scripture is inspired by God and profitable for teaching, for reproof, for correction, for training in righteousness; that the man of God may be adequate, equipped for every good work." Through Scripture, we can learn about God's character. As we read the Bible, we need to be like a sponge and soak up all He has to tell us. And then, as we go through our days, we need to listen to the Holy Spirit as He shows us how to apply God's words in our daily life.

Another way we can learn about God is through other Believers He puts in our lives. There is nothing like a Christian brother or sister who comes along side us and encourages us with God's words. Such encouragement spurs us along in our faith. Whether it be a Scripture that we need to help us through the challenges of life, or a reminder from a fellow Believer that God always keeps His promises, God always gives us what we need, exactly when we need it.

3...Pruning for Our Good

Good morning! I love feeling fall in the air. I'm able to be outside more to enjoy God's beauty. Just a couple of weeks before Alan died, he planted two rose bushes in front of our house. He said I deserved roses every day and so this was his way of giving them to me. He was sweet that way. I've pruned the rose bushes several times to help them grow stronger.

As I was pruning them yesterday, I was reminded about how God does the same thing with us. John 15:2 tells us why God prunes us. "Every branch [aka ... Believers] in Me that does not bear fruit, He takes away; and every branch that bears fruit, He prunes it, that it may bear more fruit." I prune my rose bushes by removing dead branches and trimming back the good branches to allow them to grow more blooms. God prunes us so that we too would bear more fruit. If you're not producing fruit, He doesn't cut you back, which is pruning, — He cuts you off. Ouch! Sometimes seasons of being pruned are not comfortable because God gets rid of whatever is keeping us from producing more fruit. That might mean He will ask us to give up some things or even relationships. God wants us to be everything He designed us to be so He will get rid of anything in the way of that ultimate goal. Our God is The Master Gardener. He knows how much to prune and the best time in our lives to do the pruning to achieve His desired results of producing fruit that makes Him happy, which in turn should make us happy. So when we find ourselves being pruned, don't fight it. God is taking what is good and making it better!

3

4...Dancing in the Rain

Good morning! "Life isn't about how to survive the storm but how to dance in the rain." This saying is embroidered on a towel in my kitchen. I have to chuckle every time I change my decorative towels. You see, I have a towel rack that hooks over one of my lower kitchen cabinets. Alan always told me to hang the towel that I **didn't** want him to actually use on that rack and that way he'd never mess it up. ☺

In life, there's always going to be messes. We are guaranteed to have problems. John 16:33 tells us so. "These things I have spoken to you, that in Me you may have peace. In the world you have tribulation, but take courage; I have overcome the world." Jesus warns us that we should expect to have trouble in this life. But He has also told us that we can have peace despite our trials. The peace that Jesus refers to will come when we keep our eyes on Him and not on the trouble we are facing.

The Christian singer, David Crowder, sings a song, *Come as You Are*, that says the same thing that Jesus tells us. The lyrics say that, "Earth has no sorrows that Heaven can't heal." Then the next line tells us what to do with our troubles. "So, lay down your burdens." This song is such a good reminder that we need to keep lifting our face to the Lord and just focus on Him. That is how we can dance in the rain and survive the storms. This is my prayer for us today and always.

5...The Right Path

Good morning! Have you noticed how the morning dew refreshes our plants and flowers outside? About five years ago, during one of my hospital stays, the kids sent me a floral arrangement. Along with the fresh flowers was a small plant. The plant had purple leaves and every morning, small pink flowers would bloom. They'd only stay open for a couple of hours, so you had to get up early to see the blooms. When the flowers wilted, we took the plant and planted it in its own pot. Over the years, we've kept dividing the plant. Now I have four pots of them hanging on my porch. In late fall, I'll bring them inside and hang them in my mud room for the winter. They are the heartiest plants I've ever seen.

As I was watering them, I thought of the verses in Lamentations 3:22-23: "The Lord's lovingkindnesses indeed never cease, for His compassions never fail. They are new every morning; great is Thy faithfulness." No matter what kind of a day you had yesterday, today is a new day, a fresh start. God's mercy refreshes us just like the morning dew refreshes the plants. It doesn't matter if you missed the mark by a mile yesterday or only by a bit, God gives us a new start each day.

I don't know about you, but there have been many days that I thank the Lord that the day is over because I know tomorrow has to be better. The best way to start each new day is by being in God's Word. I know mornings can be hectic but if you would give the Lord a few minutes, He will bless that time you spend with Him and start your day on the right path ... the one leading straight to the Father!

6...Moving Our Puzzle Pieces

Good morning! "Out of sight, out of mind." God doesn't want us to live in the past but from time to time it's good to reflect on what God has brought us through. We often can see God's hand at work in our lives a bit clearer once some time has passed. Seeing His handprints on everything that I thought was terrible at the time puts wind underneath my wings. Life sometimes seems like a gigantic jigsaw puzzle, with some major pieces missing. But I can promise you that those pieces aren't lost, God just hasn't shown you where they belong yet.

Take a situation in your life where you clearly saw God's hands all over it. Now step back and look at all the things that had to happen to bring you to this place. Those things are the puzzle pieces. It's mind-boggling how God can orchestrate everything the way He does. Sometimes it's hard to see God working in our lives. When that happens, we can still be at peace because without a shadow of a doubt, He's moving the necessary puzzle pieces around for our benefit and His glory.

One of my favorite verses dealing with waiting on the Lord is Isaiah 40:31:

> *Yet those who wait for the Lord will gain new strength; they will mount up with wings like eagles, they will run and not get tired, they will walk and not become weary.*

So how is your puzzle looking? As we wait to see more pieces revealed, we can rest with 100% assurance that God is indeed moving in our lives. He is perfectly fitting together each piece of your puzzle … in His perfect timing.

7...Singing His Praises

Good morning! Since yesterday was a rainy day, I spent some down time looking through pictures on my computer and I camped out in the folder from one of our excursions to Amidon State Park. It's located near Fredericktown, Missouri. It was only about a 45-minute drive for us and the drive itself was always pretty. It is one of those hidden treasures and most times we were the only ones there.

Alan and I loved going there to climb on the pink granite rocks and listen to the water rush over them. It's a very relaxing place to go for a couple of hours. As I was thanking God for this beautiful area He gave us to go to, I was reminded of the verses in Luke that talked about if **we** didn't sing praises to God, the **rocks** would.

Luke 19:37-40 says:

> *And as He was now approaching near the descent of the Mount of Olives, the whole multitude of the disciples began to praise God joyfully with a loud voice for all the miracles which they had seen, saying, "Blessed is the King who comes in the name of the Lord! Peace in heaven and glory in the highest!" And some of the Pharisees in the multitude said to Him, "Teacher, rebuke Your disciples." And He answered, "I tell you, if these become silent, the stones will cry out."*

Isn't that cool? Even if we were silent, the rocks would sing out God's praises. The Lord is definitely worthy of our praises every day. So, here's to joyfully singing His praises and letting the rocks remain silent.

8...Holding Tight

Good morning! Going into the grocery store, I saw a mom and a little boy walking hand-in-hand. I thought it was so cute, until I got closer to them. Complete with sound effects, the little boy was doing his level best to get his hand out of his mom's hand. It was evident that this little tyke thought he could do this without his mom and he was ready to show it. But the mom had quite a grip on him and he wasn't getting away from her until she said so.

After I finished chuckling about what I had seen, I started thinking. Don't we do that same thing with God? We think that we can handle things on our own, so we let go of His hand and go about our business thinking we've got everything under control. We feel confident that all is good and then when a crisis comes, and some sort of crisis always hits, we realize that we can't get this one done by ourselves so we want to reach out for and hold His hand again and wonder why we ever let it go in the first place!

Isaiah 41:13 says:

> *"For I am the Lord your God, who upholds your right hand, who says to you, do not fear I will help you."*

Just like the mother didn't want to let go of that little boy's hand, our Heavenly Father wants to hang on to our hand, too, knowing that this would be the best thing for us. Life would be so much easier if we just remembered to take hold of God's hand and not let go. So, here's to holding tight!

9...Speak What You Believe

Good morning! Have you ever read verses in the Bible and just as soon as you let those words sink in, the Holy Spirit shows you something that you need to fix? This recently happened to me as I was reading Ephesians 3:20-21.

> *Now to Him who is able to do exceedingly abundantly beyond all that we ask or think, according to the power that works within us, to Him be the glory in the church and in Christ Jesus to all generations forever and ever. Amen.*

I have camped out on these verses since Alan died.

Last night I realized that what I was praying wasn't the same thing I was saying to others. If we pray with a doubt in our mind that God will answer that prayer, we aren't honoring Him in our prayers. Mark 11:24 tells us that if we believe God can grant us what we've asked Him for, then we will receive that answer to prayer. The caveat to that statement is that our prayer has to be something that God can answer and stay true to His character. When we pray, we need not say, "Lord, if you can help me out with this one I'd appreciate it." Of course, He can help us out with what we need! He has access to all the resources in the world. There's no "if" about it. As issues pop up in our lives, we can confidently go to the Lord and ask for what we need. Believing that He will answer that prayer honors Him. Then when we talk to others about the need, we need to speak with the same confidence that we had when we asked God to intervene. By doing this, problems that would have thrown us in a tail spin no longer can derail us. Hope will rush in to replace discouragement and trust will erase doubt. So here's to keeping our focus on the One who can take care of us and all our needs.

10...Looking Up

Good morning! Have you ever traveled in a motor home? If not, could I suggest you put that one on your Bucket List? It's cool to be able to get up and fix a drink or get a snack while you are still going down the road, or even use the restroom. Besides the comfort of traveling in one, you sit up so high when you ride in a motor home that you see things from a whole new perspective.

As I was noticing things I wouldn't have been able to see if I was traveling in a car, I thought about how God sees things. When He looks down on all His creations, He sees things from a unique vantage point that we will never have. He can look above all our circumstances because He sees the bigger picture.

God encourages us to see things the way He does. He wants us to let the light of His presence fill us so that we view the world through His eyes. Jesus said in John 8:12:

"I am the light of the world; he who follows Me shall not walk in the darkness, but shall have the light of life."

It wouldn't be practical for us to ride around town in a motor home to run our errands, but we can still keep that same perspective by simply looking up. Looking down or at our challenges doesn't produce a good fix to our problems. It's only when we look up to our Heavenly Father that we can maintain the right perspective. So, here's to keeping our eyes fixed on the One who sits higher than all!

11...Tightening Our Belts

Good morning! Are you the type of person that can laugh at yourself? I am and I not only provided laughter for myself but gave my friends last week quite a chuckle, too. OK, so when you fly fish, you wear waders to keep you dry as you stand in waist or chest deep water to fish. Sometimes it is difficult to change positions in moving water. The last day of fishing, I was standing in waist high water when I needed to take a step backwards. When I did, I fell in a hole causing water to rush inside my waders. Oh boy, that'll get your attention in a hurry! Did I mention that this water is extremely cold??!! Until that happened, I did not know the purpose of the belt I was wearing. You wear a safety belt so if you would accidentally get any water inside your waders, you can still get out of the water safely because they won't fill up completely with water. But the belt needed to be pulled much tighter than I had it pulled to work correctly. My friends tried not to laugh but it was pretty funny watching me pour water out of my waders, wring the water out of my socks ... you get the picture. Later, I was comforted by the fact that if you've been trout fishing very long, you'll know that this happens to the best of them.

Having equipment but not using it correctly doesn't help you. Having a Bible prominently displayed in your home but never opening it won't help you either. God's word brings life to our soul. It's a love story like no other. It's also our guide for life. God's word helps us learn how to live a life pleasing to Him. Psalm 119:105 says, "Thy word is a lamp to my feet, and a light to my path." So, my prayer for us today, is that we'd stay safe as we encounter the pitfalls in life by tightening our belts through God's word.

12...CAN DO!

Good morning! As I was reading in Galatians last night, God showed me something new. Don't you just love how He does that? You can read the same passage over and over again and then the next time you read it, God shows you something you hadn't seen before. I shouldn't be surprised because the Bible is the Living Word of God. Anyway, here are the verses I read in Galatians 5:22-23:

> *But the fruit of the Spirit is love, joy, peace, patience, kindness, goodness, faithfulness, gentleness, self-control; against such things there is no law.*

It's the fruit of self-control that got my attention this time. I've always associated the things that we shouldn't do as the self-control things. You know, like having enough self-control so you don't lash out in anger, or push away from the table so you don't eat too much, or keep your mouth in check so you don't have to apologize later for your words spoken in haste.

But last night I started looking at self-control as things I *should* be doing. Things like having enough self-control to put down that TV remote, and pick up the Bible to read or to call a friend to focus on their issues instead of our own. In life, aren't we more apt to do the things on the "can do" list over the "don't do" list? So, as I go through today, I'm going to focus on the "can do" of self-control and see how many things I can add to that list. Hope you'll join me.

13...Consider the Source

Good morning! When I was little and someone would say something unkind to me, usually a mean comment about my speech problems, my dad would always say, "Consider the source." As a kid, I never totally understood the point he was trying to make, but I get it now. If you've lived any years at all, you know that everyone has an opinion about everything. Some people believe that everyone they come in contact with needs to hear their opinion. I think the important thing we need to consider is what we do with our opinions. The negative opinions of others can sidetrack us in an instant, if we value what they say more than what we know is true through the Lord. We don't need to consider any source that doesn't line up with God's word. Opinions that try to sway us away from what God has instructed us to do are not opinions we need to listen to.

You can normally tell within minutes of talking with someone if they are a positive or a negative person. I think what my dad was trying to tell me was the same thing we read about in Matthew 7:13-29. In these verses, Jesus was explaining how you could tell if people were His followers. He said you would know by the fruits of their lives. Both my Heavenly Father and my earthly father were telling me to stick with those people bearing good fruit and steer clear of the rotten ones. So, what sources are you listening to? May I suggest that you carefully select the people in your life that you go to for advice. We need people that will encourage us with good, positive, and Godly wisdom. We need to surround ourselves with those fellow Believers that bear good fruit. My prayer for us is that we will be one of those people who lift others up!

14...KEEPING YOUR EYES WIDE OPEN

Good morning! Have you ever wanted to put up a huge "DO NOT ENTER" sign? Where I live, there is a Highway 61-Yard Sale the week before Labor Day, which stretches out for *miles* in Southeast Missouri. This annual event creates havoc for those living near Highway 61. The entrance to my private lane has an open area where there is a row of mailboxes. This area became a parking lot for many of the shoppers. After a trip to town, I was trying to turn in my lane but it was blocked by cars. Thankfully, one of the cars had a driver in it and he moved his car so I could pull in off the highway. All you can do about this extra traffic is just try to avoid it.

I was thinking about the things in life we try to avoid. When God closes a door of opportunity for us, we often try to avoid where He wants to take us and instead go ahead and park where we want to go. It's true that God usually doesn't put up a huge "Do Not Enter" sign in front of us, but if we are watching, His signs are just as clear. We must remember that our human reasoning isn't what we need to rely on. Proverbs 3:5 tells us to "Trust in the Lord with all your heart, and do not lean on your own understanding." If we trust that God will only direct us down pathways that are good for us, we could eliminate lots of stress in our lives. If we would listen closely for the Holy Spirit to prompt us in the direction we should go, it would be much easier to stay on that perfect course that God has laid out for us. Just as certain as I am that the weekend before Labor Day each year will be the Highway 61-Yard Sale, I can say with confidence that when God closes one door, He will indeed open up a new door of opportunity for you. Here's to keeping our eyes wide open in order to see where the Lord is leading us to next!

15...Whatever!

Good morning! Another beautiful day has begun. What are you thinking about already this morning? Is it something good or something troublesome? Maybe you heard something on the news that brought fear to your heart or maybe it's a lingering problem that has stressed you out. You go to sleep thinking about it and you wake up with it on your mind.

Our thoughts are so important as they determine our actions and reactions. You can't be scared to death at the same time you're overflowing with joy. Fear is something we all deal with from time to time but it's not something God wants us to hold on to. He doesn't want us hanging on to it like it's our best friend. Dwelling on the negative doesn't get us anywhere. True, there will be plenty of things in life that we just don't like. But that's where our faith comes in.

Trusting God to get us through these tough or fearful times is the only positive way to handle these issues. So, what does God want us to focus our thoughts on? Philippians 4:8 gives us that answer:

> *Finally, brethren, whatever is true, whatever is honorable, whatever is right, whatever is pure, whatever is lovely, whatever is of good repute, if there is any excellence and if anything worthy of praise, let your mind dwell on these things.*

Dwelling on these positives will indeed change our outlook. If you're struggling with something negative, give the "whatevers" a try. God knows what He's talking about when He tells us to focus on the good.

16...God's Amazing Family

Good morning! Having our family around is one of those things I think we often take for granted. We live our lives as though we have all the time in the world to visit with them ... later. And then our busy lives go on and "later" just keeps getting pushed back. But as my family unfortunately knows all too well, later isn't always given to us.

Over the weekend, I got to spend some time with Alan's mom's family at a reunion in the park. It was so nice to see all of them again. At one point, I stepped back and just watched everyone talking, laughing, playing with the little ones, taking pictures, and enjoying a meal together. I know this is what God intends a family to be like, a group of people loving and supporting one another and including everyone. It sure made my heart smile knowing Alan would have loved this gathering and it was almost like he was there with us. But even more than Alan would have enjoyed it, God loved it. Where we had about thirty-five family members at our small reunion, God's family is huge!

John 1:12 tells us who is in God's family. "But to all who did receive Him, who believed in His name, He gave the right to become children of God." Some people have tons of "friends" on social media but those numbers do not hold a candle to the number of members in God's family, both here on earth and in Heaven. I'm sure Alan is still meeting family members up there, since everyone in Heaven is family. So, let's make it a priority to make time for those we love and do our part to bring someone else into God's amazing family.

17...LASTING COMFORT

Good morning! When things aren't running smoothly in our life, don't we run to comfort? For lots of us, we turn to people we love when we are in need of comfort. Others, turn to food, like chocolate or ice cream, to comfort them. And yet others find their comfort in a place, like a favorite location.

While these "comfort-givers" can give us temporary comfort, there's a real problem with turning to any of them. They are all just temporary fixes. People will leave us, food will be consumed, and a place will only be good while you are at that location. Then what??

If we want real and lasting comfort, there's only one way to get it. Go straight to the God of all comfort. 2 Corinthians 1:3-5 states:

> *Blessed be the God and Father of our Lord Jesus Christ, the Father of mercies and the God of all comfort; who comforts us in all our affliction so that we may be able to comfort those who are in any affliction with the comfort with which we ourselves are comforted by God. For just as the sufferings of Christ are ours in abundance, so also our comfort is abundant through Christ.*

God is always with us throughout every moment of every day. He sees all, hears all, and knows all. He can provide us with greater comfort than we can even imagine. Turning to God is the only way I've found lasting comfort. Only with His divine comfort, can it be said, "It is well, with my soul." Praying you find lasting comfort in Him, too.

18...Needing Others

Good morning! Have you ever noticed that we seem to spend time with groups of people? We gravitate to those with a common thread that links us together. For example, all the ladies in one of the Bible studies I was in were all widows. I have dinners as often as I can with ladies I taught school with. Guys hang out with fellow hunters or fishermen and families hang out with other families that their kids are in sports together. There are all kinds of support groups people can also get involved in. There are cancer survivor groups, and on the other end of that spectrum, there are grief sharing groups to help those that have lost loved ones.

These support groups definitely line up with Scripture. Galatians 6:2 tells us to, "Bear one another's burdens, and thus fulfill the law of Christ." Hebrews 13:16 says, "And do not neglect doing good and sharing; for with such sacrifices God is pleased." And Philippians 2:4 tells us to "not merely look out for your own personal interests, but also for the interests of others."

I am so thankful God created us to need others. We were never intended to live this life alone and I'm grateful to share this life with so many people. But the day I'm looking forward to the most is that day in which the common thread that joins us together is Jesus. Just like the song says ...

When we all get to Heaven,
what a day of rejoicing that will be!
When we all see Jesus,
we'll sing and shout the victory!

Until then ...

19...Let Them Out

Good morning! Have you ever experienced the "box effect?" You know, when someone is almost branded to be a certain way. We stick them in a box and give them no room to grow or change. We have certain low expectations of them based on past performances of some kind. Whether it be once self-centered, always self-centered; once a total jerk, always a jerk; once a liar, always a liar; once considered lazy, always lazy; once irresponsible, always irresponsible; and the list could go on for pages. The one very important thing missing in these examples is the power of God. Any of the above examples could be changed with God's help.

As Christians, we should be growing and changing every day. 2 Corinthians 3:18 says, "But we all, with unveiled face beholding as in a mirror the glory of the Lord, are being transformed into the same image from glory to glory, just as from the Lord, the Spirit." So, if our precious Lord can take us, past sins and all, and daily transform us into the image of Jesus, then why do we try to keep others in the box of what used to define them? If we don't let them out of their "box," then why would we ever expect God to allow us to get out of our box? I don't know about you, but I'm so very thankful that God doesn't box me up because of my bad choices of the past. He has picked me up, brushed me off, and guided me in the direction of an abundant life in Him. So today, is there someone that you need to let out of their box? My prayer is that we would realize when we're boxing someone up and quickly change our mindset about that individual and be ready to watch who they can become in Jesus.

20...God's Value

Good morning! "Beauty is in the eye of the beholder." I recently had my home and land appraised. It was weird for me to have someone looking over what I have and putting a value on it because there are so many variables when it comes to determining a value. The appraised amount is partially based on the value of what others in my area have. What's crazy is that the value is subject to change based on what other homes and land sell for. Things are so subjective that two appraisers can appraise the same home and come up with different values.

While the appraiser's numbers can change, I'm thankful that the value the Lord places on His children NEVER changes. As Scripture tells us, He loves us so much that while we were still sinners, Jesus died for us. Romans 5:8 says it this way, "But God demonstrates His own love towards us, and that while we were yet sinners, Christ died for us." Now that's a love we can always count on.

Something else that will never change is the Bible. Once we realize the worth of Scripture, we no longer read it just so we can check it off our list of something we need to do. Instead, we consider it to be the fuel that our body needs. God's love and His Word are never subject to change. It doesn't matter how much the world changes; they remain the same. God's love and His word are the beauty in the eye of this beholder, helping to navigate me through this life. Praying they are the same for you!

21...Don't Open the Door

Good morning! I have a little fall display at my house. It consists of a bale of hay with mums and pumpkins in front of it. A couple of my pumpkins are green and they look just like an apple. You guessed it … they are called apple pumpkins. Although the outsides are different, they are what you'd expect a pumpkin to be on the inside. I had to trash one of the pumpkins already. When I picked it up, I found that it was rotten on the bottom. And upon further investigation, I discovered that the inside of the pumpkin was rotten too, even though the outside still looked good. It made me think about how in life we often try to disguise sin by wrapping it up in something that looks appealing or pleasing. But when you take the cover off, the sin remains. You might be able to conceal the sin for a time, but just like how the pumpkin rotted, sin that is left unchecked in our lives will start a decaying process in us and lessen our witness for God.

Paul tells us in Ephesians 4:27 that we should not give Satan an open door to enter into our lives. "And do not give the devil an opportunity." The enemy gets that opportunity when we try to cover up our sin instead of dealing with it head on. Satan is just a big bully. Once he gets one foot in the door of our life, he makes himself at home, where he keeps doing more damage, and we begin to drift a little further from the Lord. The good news is that there is a way to put this bully in his place. And that way is through Jesus. James 4:7 tells us that if we will resist the devil, he will flee from us. My prayer for us is that we don't allow the enemy to put even a toe in our life. Instead, I pray that we keep our focus on the One we want to 100% fill our lives … Jesus!!

22...Mold Me

Good morning! As I was looking through some pictures, I found a picture of Alan and I that had been taken seven years ago at Silver Dollar City in Branson, Missouri. We went there to celebrate our birthdays. We both turned 50 that year and so did Silver Dollar City. We were sitting in a sleigh in front of one of their huge Christmas trees. Such good memories. One thing we enjoyed there was watching craftsman at their trade. My favorite craftsman was a potter making clay pots. As he worked at the wheel, he'd take a lump of clay and mold it into a beautiful and unique pot. He took his time perfecting that pot, patiently smoothing out all the rough spots and imperfections. It was amazing to see what he could create out of a lump of clay.

It reminded me of the verse in Isaiah talking about God being the Divine Potter. Isaiah 64:8 says, "But now, O Lord, Thou art our Father, we are the clay, and Thou our potter; and all of us are the work of Thy hand." Just like the potter we saw in Branson, God is very patient with us, smoothing out our imperfections, which will one day mold us into that perfect vessel that He designed us to be.

All of us are a unique creation with the same goal of being transformed into the image of Christ. I guess the question we need to answer is, "Are we willing to let the Divine Potter mold us into a beautiful vessel or will we fight that process and remain an imperfect lump of clay?"

Here's to letting God smooth out our flaws!

23...Getting Rid of the Ashes

Good morning! As it gets closer to the end of October, we tend to hear about lots of hay rides and bonfires going on. I was thinking about those bonfires as I was picking up sticks and yard debris and throwing them in my fire pit to burn. When my fire finally burned out, all that remained were ashes. I took those ashes and tossed them aside as they had no value to me. I was reminded about those ashes when I read 1 Corinthians 3:12-15.

Now if any man builds upon the foundation with gold, silver, precious stones, wood, hay, straw, each man's work will become evident; for the day will show it, because it is to be revealed with fire; and the fire itself will test the quality of each man's work. If any man's work which has been built upon it remains, he shall receive a reward. If any man's work is burned up, he shall suffer loss; but he himself shall be saved, yet so as through fire.

As believers, we know that our salvation is a free gift but the Heavenly rewards that we get once we are in Heaven depend on the Kingdom work we do here. Those works will be put through the fire and our good works for the Kingdom will remain and those that were not pleasing to the Lord will burn up and only ashes will remain. Those ashes will be tossed aside, just like I did with my fire pit ashes, and whatever works remain will be rewarded. Here on earth, I only want ashes as the end result of my fire. But in Heaven, when my works are tested by fire, I want as few ashes as possible to remain. Hope this is your goal, too!

24...Peace vs. Chaos

Good morning! We have several feral cats at our place, a baker's dozen to be exact. The other day when my granddaughter was here, she accidentally let one get inside the house. I was able to get the cat cornered in my bedroom and closed the door. As it freaked out, it pulled down some blinds, knocked almost everything off my nightstand and the same with the dresser. That stupid thing decided it was going to camp out underneath the dresser. So, I had to go to Plan B.

As I was getting the leaf blower out of the garage, my son and his family pulled up. Of course, he wanted to know what I was doing with the leaf blower so I quickly filled him in. When I returned to my bedroom, I stuck the leaf blower under the dresser and turned it on high. That cat came flying out from the back of the dresser and ran crazy through the room again, but this time my son was able to grab him and boot him outside.

Do you ever have chaos in your life???? It seems like the chaos in our lives always comes when we absolutely don't have time for it. You know, when our schedules are so busy you almost have to pencil-in sleeping. How many times have you caught yourself saying, "Seriously, I don't have time for this?" But John 14:27 tells us that Jesus left us a valuable gift to combat the chaos ... His peace. Regardless of our situations in life, His peace is always available for the taking. He is NEVER too busy to extend His peace to us. That concept of never being too busy for us boggles my mind since there are a gazillion people He offers that peace to. So, my prayer is that we accept this beautiful gift He gives us. Here's to worshiping the Prince of Peace!

25...Making Memories

Good morning! I've been doing a lot of reminiscing lately. Do you ever do that? Just spending some time going over in your head how things were at different times in your life? I've been thinking about things that warmed my heart as a child, and there were lots of them. Times with my parents and the lessons I learned from them. Crazy stuff with my siblings that have happened over the years. Times with my girlfriends that will stay with me forever. And all the ways Alan loved me that will be forever etched in my heart.

On tough days, those memories make my heart smile. It's as if the memories make my heart do the Happy Dance. And when your heart is happy, everything seems better. As great as those memories are, I stopped and asked myself what memories I was making with Jesus as I walk with Him every day. I could make an endless list of all the ways He has blessed me but that's about what He's given me.

What things am I giving Him? When He thinks of me, am I warming His heart? When I finally see Him face to face, will He remind me of a time when we …? I want Him to know that when I do things, I'm doing them for Him. Colossians 3:23 says, "Whatever you do, do your work heartily, as for the Lord rather than for men." So lately, before I do something for others, I just simply tell Him and remind myself that "Lord, this is for you." When I'm walking in Heaven with Jesus, I want Him to be able to put His arm around me and tell me of a time when I warmed His heart. So, what memories are you making?

26...Perspectives

Good morning! What sounds better to you, $9.99 or $10? What about 365 days or one year? It's all about your perspective, isn't it? Have you ever wondered why some people refuse to accept the Lord's invitation for salvation, especially with how crazy this world is becoming? For those of us who have accepted the gift of salvation and know that Heaven is our forever home, it's often hard for us to understand why anyone would want anything but that.

Before we accepted the path that Jesus made possible for us, we most likely had the same false perceptions as those who haven't accepted Jesus yet. Do you remember some of your perceptions at that time? You might have thought things like you could never see yourself as being good enough or you thought that God would never forgive your wheel barrel full of sins. And maybe you thought if you became a Christian, the days of you having any fun would be over. But then, someone came along side you and started speaking truths in your life and you started wondering if maybe your perceptions had been wrong. As Believers, we are the living example of Christ. Those who have yet to come to faith watch us carefully to see if our words match up with our actions. 1 Peter 3:15 says, "but sanctify Christ as Lord in your hearts, always being ready to make a defense to everyone who asks you to give an account for the hope that is in you ..." We are here on this earth to further God's kingdom. Just like someone helped us see God's perception on life and death, we are called to be ready to help others see life from God's point of view. Are you prepared to do that? I pray we will always be ready and sitting on "Go"!

27...Train Them Up

Good morning! We've all heard the saying that imitation is the sincerest form of flattery, but that's not always the case. Yesterday as I was waiting to see my doctor, a woman and four kids came into the waiting room. Within a few minutes of their conversation, one of the kids started loudly giving his responses. The real problem wasn't that his voice was too loud, but what he was saying. Let's just say if that language was used in a movie, it would have to be R-rated. The mother quickly let the rest of us know that he was not her child but a friend's child that she was babysitting.

It was a great reminder that it makes a difference what we do and say around children. They observe our behavior and hear our words and often repeat them. You don't have to be their parents or grandparents to make a difference either. It can be a neighborhood child, or your friend's kids, or just a child you see a lot. Since we know that children look up to adults, we need to be aware of our surroundings and who is in earshot of what we are saying and choose our words carefully.

Proverbs 22:6 says, "Train up a child in the way he should go, even when he is old he will not depart from it." As adults, we have a wonderful opportunity to influence the next generation for Jesus. So, here's to choosing our words and actions carefully, especially around children, and giving them something good to imitate!

28...In God We Trust

Good morning! When I was little, there was a cute little chant we'd say when we saw a penny on the ground. "Find a penny, pick it up, all day long you'll have good luck." When I was putting groceries in my car, I saw three pennies on the ground and "the kid" in me picked them up. Of course, that familiar saying went through my head. I picked the pennies up and looked to see what year was on them, something Alan got me doing, and then I was reminded about what was inscribed on the coins, "In God We Trust."

Is that inscription something we do all the time? How about when life comes raining down on us with hurricanes, fires, or earthquakes? Or what about when the doctor's report isn't what we prayed for? And do we trust when relationships are strained or even ended? Our founding fathers knew that to live this life, we needed to put our trust in the Lord ALL the time and in EVERY situation.

Psalm 20:7 addresses the trust we need to have in the Lord. "Some boast [trust] in chariots, and some in horses; but we will boast [trust] in the name of the Lord, our God." For our era, that verse could be written as ..."Some trust in their own power, and some in their money; but we will trust in the name of the Lord, our God." You could easily replace those things we trust in, to lots of other things the world boasts, or trusts in, but the last part of that Scripture will never change ... we will trust in the name of the Lord, our God! What or who do you place your trust in? Praying your answer is always JESUS!

29...Blessed Assurance

Good morning! As I was watching the weather forecast on TV, I was again amazed how they can determine what the weather will be like over a week away. Even more amazing is the fact that the Farmer's Almanac predicts the weather a year in advance. Now it's true that their predictions aren't always accurate, but they're close. I can't tell you what will happen in the next hour, let alone next year but I know someone who can. You guessed it ... God.

Even though God doesn't show us in advance everything that will happen throughout our lives, I am confident in the plans He has for us because Jeremiah 29:11 says, "'For I know the plans that I have for you,' declares the Lord, 'plans for welfare and not for calamity to give you a future and a hope.'"

Then as I was flipping through Jeremiah, I found this verse in Chapter 17, verse 7. "Blessed is the man who trusts **in** the Lord and whose trust **is** the Lord." We all look for certainties in life. It helps us deal with the things that come our way. If I had no other assurance but those two verses, I wouldn't need to worry about what lies ahead for me in the future because God has already figured it out and He's the One that can make it good. We can be confident and rest in the Lord knowing He has great plans ahead for our lives. Here's to seeing what God has in store for us!

30...Seeing Their Hearts

Good morning! I was walking down memory lane and it took me to the deli that Alan and I owned. I have so many great memories there. Because of the deli, I met some amazing people and this Veteran's Day reminded me of one of them.

The deli operated on the honor system. Once people had finished eating, they just came to the register, told us what they had, and paid us. It was there at the register that I saw people's hearts. It was at the register that people would ask to anonymously pay for someone's meal or even for an entire table of people. I got to see the giver and the excitement they had to do something nice for someone else. And I got to see the receiver's face when they came up to pay their bill and I was able to tell them they didn't owe anything because someone else had already paid for their food. Those are those priceless moments that I will carry with me always.

It's that "putting your money where your mouth is," that brought up memories today. Every year on Veteran's Day, a guy who we were so proud to call our friend, gave us money to buy as many meals for veterans that day as he could. That was his way of anonymously saying "thank you" to the veterans for their service. Some veterans would get teary-eyed when they came to the register and we were able to extend our friend's thank you for their service. 1 Peter 4:10 tells us that we are to serve one another as good stewards out of what God has given us. There's all kinds of ways we can serve our brothers and sisters, but some of my favorite ways were things that I saw take place at the deli. So, as we honor our veterans today, I pray you find your own way to say, "Thank you."

31...Overflowing

Good morning! Don't you just love those days when you wake up and realize that you don't have any set plans and you can just let the day flow? Well, my day did flow ... right over the top of the toilet and onto the bathroom floor. Not exactly what I had in mind as I thought about my carefree day. This situation is what Alan called the "joys of homeownership." This toilet issue wasn't a major problem, just more of an inconvenience. Nothing that a trip to the hardware store wouldn't fix. As I was attempting to stop this overflow, I broke the plunger. They just don't make them like they used to. Either that, or it was an operator error. LOL ☺ I had to chuckle as I was mopping the floor because I was thinking about the irony of Alan calling it the "joy" of homeownership. But it actually makes a lot of sense when you think about it. Because you own it, you take joy in taking what's broken and restoring it.

It's the same way with our relationship with God. He is in the restoration business. Once we accept His gift of salvation, He takes our sins and forgives us; takes our emptiness and fills us; and takes our fears and replaces them with hope. In Psalm 23, David reminds us that our Great Shepherd provides all we need and that He not only protects us, but He is our constant companion. With that being so, my prayer is that our lives would overflow with all the blessings that the Lord has for us. May our cups runneth over!

32...Healthy Diet

Good morning! Many people make yearly resolutions and one of the resolutions that is typically made each year is to lose weight. People go and sign up for gym memberships or enroll in exercise classes. A commitment is made to eat healthier, even though it costs more money to do so. We start out strong and then within a short period of time, we stop going to the gym and attending those classes for a gazillion different reasons. We tell ourselves we'll just exercise at home since it's much easier to fit that into our schedule. Then we make ourselves feel better by saying that eating healthier will make a big difference in our weight just by itself. Does this sound familiar???

So, how is your diet looking? I'm not asking about the physical food we take in, but the spiritual food. Just like your body needs healthy food every day, your soul needs to be fed daily, too. 1 Peter 2:2 says we should *want* to spend time in God's Word. "Like newborn babies, long for the pure milk of the word, that by it you may grow in respect to salvation."

Both diets, physical and spiritual, will suffer greatly without the proper food. And just like the excuses we come up with for not following through on the resolutions to lose weight, we can come up with just as many excuses to justify why we can't feed our souls. If your schedule is too full to focus on both, then I'd suggest picking the one with eternal ramifications ... your spiritual diet. So, here's to daily feeding our souls!

33...Our Forever Home

Good morning! As my neighbor said this weekend, I'm getting things at my house ready for winter. Doing things like putting the garden hoses away, taking care of the outdoor plants, having the house pressured washed and getting flower beds ready to plant my mums. I'm just trying to be a good steward of what God has blessed me with here on earth.

As nice as the home the Lord has given me here, I must remember that this is not my forever home. We are all just passing through here on earth, with our final destination being either Heaven or hell for all eternity, whichever place you choose. Yes, you pick the destination. James 4:14 says that "you are just a vapor that appears for a little while and then vanishes away." Our life here on earth is just a temporary residence. Scripture tells us that we have a set number of days to live on earth, and since this life is so short, we need to closely look at what we are doing to prepare for our forever home.

So, the question that needs to be answered is, "Do you have your earthly house in order, not just for the winter season, but for all seasons?" When this life is over, and no one knows when that time will come, the only thing that will matter is whether or not we have a personal relationship with God through Jesus. You are the only one who can make this life-changing choice and it must be made while we are here on earth. So, if you haven't yet made that crucial decision, there is no better day than today to ask Jesus to be your Lord and Savior. I pray you choose the same final destination as I have, as I wouldn't want to celebrate and live forever in Heaven without you!

34...Perfect Love

Good morning! One of my new favorite places is Bennett Spring State Park. It's nature in its finest. Everywhere you look, you can see God's masterpieces. "A picture paints a thousand words" is a saying that people use when words just can't adequately explain the beauty they are seeing. That would be true about the beauty that is so prevalent at Bennett Spring.

Another one of God's masterpieces is something we haven't seen yet, but Alan has ... it's Heaven. The Bible gives us some glimpses as to what Heaven looks like in Revelation. We read about streets of pure gold that look like transparent glass and how every kind of precious stone will be found there. But even though that beauty would be hard to put into words, the picture I can't wait to see deals with those people who will be living there.

When you look at the news these days, there are all kinds of examples of people not being able to tolerate other people. In many cases, this intolerance leads to violence but in Heaven there will be perfect harmony. Nothing will exist except perfect love for one another. Can you imagine that? I think God uses nature to show us the beauty and harmony He wants for us all. I can't wait to see the perfection that awaits all believers in Heaven! What about you?

35...Stand Boldly

Good morning! I really love the winter season. And no, it's not just because I love snow but it's because I love tennis. While we are having colder temps here, Australia is heating up, as it's their summer season. As I was watching one of the tournaments leading up to the Australian Open, I began reflecting on how tennis is as much a mental game as it is a skills game. Other players will look at you like you look at yourself. Are you confident as a player or do you think you don't belong on the same court with a player that's ranked much higher than you are?

We could ask that same question in our Christian walk. Do you see yourself as a child of God? And if that question doesn't blow your mind, try this one. Do you see yourself as fellow heirs with Christ? Romans 8:17 tells us just that. We are "fellow heirs with Christ." Can you imagine what life would be like if we really saw ourselves as God sees us? And not only if we saw ourselves as God sees us, but if we lived life accordingly.

I believe that is how we can experience a piece of Heaven on earth. So today my prayer is that we stand a little straighter, hold our head up high, and remind ourselves that God loves us so much as Believers, that He made us fellow heirs with Christ. Now if that doesn't cause you to have a good day, nothing will!

36...Invest Wisely

Good morning! Do you ever just stop and think about the people that God has placed in your life? God is all about relationships. I know this because He made the only way we can get to Him is by a relationship with His Son, Jesus. (John 14:6) With our ultimate goal being able to spend eternity with God, and serve the Lord while we're here on this planet, our earthly relationships should reflect that goal. So what do we need to look for in our relationships? Knowing that the influence of those around us plays an important role in who we become, we should surround ourselves with people who continually spur us on to becoming more and more like Christ.

Those friends will encourage you and pray for you. They will remind you that you are a son or daughter of the King of Kings and the Lord of Lords. When life tries to tear you down, they will build you up. When you're not sure where to go next, they will pray with you until God opens a door and then they will walk beside you on the path that God has opened up for you. Their love and support will help you fulfill the plan that God has for your life.

These godly people that invest in you, want you to succeed in your faith walk. Hebrews 10:24 sums up what we are all called to do. "... and let us consider how to stimulate one another to love and good deeds." So, as we go about our day, let's focus on how we can love others and build them up in Jesus.

37...Keep Them Charged

Good morning! When we have brutally cold weather, I usually don't spend much time outside. Alan had a car that was parked outside and because I wasn't going outside much, I didn't start Alan's car on a regular basis to just let it run. I had someone who wanted to buy it during a cold snap and when I went outside to take the car for a drive, it wouldn't start. Apparently the car battery needed to be charged. After getting it hooked up with jumper cables, and letting it charge, it fired right up.

The same happens to us if we don't hook up with God for a while. When we go for a time without communicating with the Lord, we find that our spiritual battery becomes low and that it needs to be recharged. When we're not charged up, it affects every part of our life. So, what do we do when our spiritual batteries are running low? We should follow the example of Jesus and do what He did.

Luke 5:16 tell us that Jesus "would often slip away to the wilderness and pray." Jesus knew if He didn't spend time with God the Father, He wouldn't be able to minister effectively. The same is true for us. Spending quality time with the Lord is essential to living the life He has called us to live. Our busy schedules often try to interfere with our much needed time with God but I can promise you that God is the last thing we should take out of our schedules. If Jesus needed time alone with God to do His will, then rest assured we need it, too. So, here's to keeping our batteries charged!

38...Persevere

Good morning! Have you ever been forced to do something that you absolutely did not want to do, but afterwards you're glad you did it? I've been putting off a project for 16 months, but because I needed to find something that was in the closet, with the help of my sister, I cleaned out Alan's closet. As this project was underway, God began reminding me that throughout the Bible He gave many assignments that I know the people didn't want to do, but they were obedient and followed God's instructions.

In Genesis Chapter 22, God gave Abraham some mind-boggling instructions. "Take now your son, your only son, whom you love, Isaac, and go to the land of Moriah; and offer him there as a burnt offering on one of the mountains of which I will tell you." Yikes! That was some request! What would your answer have been if you were Abraham? As this story continues, Abraham did as the Lord instructed, but before Abraham took the knife to slay his son, the angel of the Lord said to Abraham, "Do not stretch out your hand against the lad, and do nothing to him; for now I know that you fear God, since you have not withheld your son, your only son, from Me." Since Abraham was obedient, God promised to bless him and his offspring. I can't imagine what must have been going through Abraham's mind as he got things ready to sacrifice Isaac, but no matter what he was thinking, he still trusted God and obeyed. So what is God calling you to do? It might be something that you're not emotionally ready to do, or it may seem harsh that you're asked to do it, but I would encourage you to do it anyway. Trusting the Lord is always the right response. And even with a small task, like what I did today, blessings will follow if you persevere.

39...Log Removal Business

Good morning! I was recently watching the Auckland tennis tournament on TV. I was absolutely amazed at what they showed one man doing as he was "supposed" to be watching the match. Keep in mind that he was sitting very close to the court so those seats were not cheap and not easy to come by. OK, ready for this??? He was reading a newspaper. I just had to shake my head. Why go through the motions if you're not interested in being there?

Observing that man made me think through how often we as Christians just go through the motions, almost as though we were checking things off a daily checklist, instead of really putting our full focus on what God has for us to do. So as crazy as it was for that spectator to be totally oblivious to what was happening with the match, I know that I've been totally disengaged with things I should've been giving my full attention to. I guess if the truth be told, we can all say that we are guilty of the same thing that I got irritated at that man over.

Why is it that we can always see other people doing stuff that just shocks us without seeing that we're no different? The last part of Luke 6:42 says, "... You hypocrite, first take the log out of your own eye, and then you will see clearly to take out the speck that is in your brother's eye." Ouch ... that sums it up in a nutshell. So, here's to being in the log removal business!

40...Boundaries

Good morning! Over the years, one thing I have loved doing with my oldest granddaughter is to sit down and color together. It's just fun to watch little ones color. The majority of the time, they don't stay within the boundaries and their color choices are random, but to them, they have created a masterpiece. In life, we set all kinds of boundaries. We put fences up in our yards to define our property lines. We use walls in our homes to separate each room. And if there are children sharing a room, they might even use tape on the floor to divide their personal space (or so I've been told).

Besides our physical boundaries, we also have spiritual boundaries. Some might think that the spiritual lines are harder to see than the physical ones, but God has given us boundary lines in which to live. Exodus 20 gives us those clear boundaries in the Ten Commandments. They are God's guidelines to abundant living. Does that mean that we will never go outside those boundaries? Nope! Just like it's a given that when young children color, they'll color outside the lines, we too will live outside of the lines that God has set for us. When we leave those safe boundaries, it is called sin. And until we reach Heaven, we will find ourselves outside the lines from time to time. God is wanting you to live as the masterpiece He created you to be. He knows that living a successful life requires boundaries and He has graciously provided those lines not to cross. Are you living within the lines that God has drawn? My prayer for us is that we would see God's boundaries as something truly beneficial. So, here's to living within the lines that are meant to help color our lives with blessings.

41...Power of Faith

Good morning! Yesterday I was reading in the book of Hebrews, Chapter 11. This chapter was talking about the power of faith in Christ. Verse 1 says, "Now faith is the assurance of things hoped for, the conviction of things not seen." And then starting in verse two, many examples of faith were given. Examples like by faith the walls of Jericho fell down, after they had been encircled for seven days, Noah by faith built the ark to save his family, by faith Sarah conceived a child in her older age, and many more examples followed in this chapter. Did you see the common thread through these examples? It was "by faith" that all these things happened. Verse 6 says, "And without faith it is impossible to please Him, for he who comes to God must believe that He is, and that He is a rewarder of those who seek Him."

These are just some of the faith examples from Scripture. When we share the hope of Jesus and explain that it is by faith we accept the gift of salvation, it would be nice to know some of these biblical "faith stories." But I think that having your own "faith stories" to share can be just as important. So, could you give some faith examples from your life? It's good to think about these things in advance so they would be easier to recall them when needed. A lot of my faith stories deal with issues of the heart ... both physical and emotional. Physical stories of how I literally laid my heart in His hands through all my heart surgeries, especially the one in which they removed a section of my heart. And the emotional heart stories deal with losses I've experienced in life and how as I stepped out in faith, God took care of me. These faith stories are our testimony of God's greatness. We need to be ready to share them whenever the Holy Spirit gives us an opportunity to do so. My prayer for us today is that we would take time to recall our personal stories so that we can one day share them with others to help bring the lost into the family of God.

42...He's Always There

Good morning! I just finished spending a week with my sister. After I took her to the airport on Saturday, I thought about the love we share as biological sisters and as Sisters in Christ. Just because she got on an airplane and flew home to Texas, doesn't mean her love left. The love we share easily spans over that distance of 500 plus miles.

That truth got me thinking about God's love and how it isn't hampered by any boundaries. Although Jesus is now physically seated at the right hand of the Father in Heaven, His spirit resides in the heart of every Believer. Being omnipresent, the Lord can be everywhere and with every Believer all at the same time. Psalm 139:7-8 says, "Where can I go from Thy Spirit? Or where can I flee from Thy presence? If I ascend to Heaven, Thou art there; if I make my bed in Sheol, behold, Thou art there." So, no matter where we are or how many miles we travel, He is always with us.

The fact that God is Spirit should bring us great comfort. He is not restricted by any borders, like we are. He is with every Believer during every moment of our lives. When we feel His presence during the day, whether we are alone or with others, that is His Spirit connecting with ours. When we feel as though we've lost connection with the Lord, which is just a "feeling" because He never leaves us, all we have to do is say His name to reconnect. Knowing that we can be connected to the Lord, every minute of every day, should give us the freedom to live boldly in Christ. I am ever so thankful that we are never without Him and for all the sisters in Christ that He has blessed my life with!

43...Sew On

Good morning! I love learning new things and this week I learned how to make a quilted potato bag. These bags allow you to get a "baked potato" in your microwave in about 4 minutes. Learning a new sewing project for me also means that there is a lot of ripping out involved until I get it all figured out.

Like many things in life, I learn more from my mistakes. The same is often true with our Christian walk. God will often need to "rip out" our efforts to make us into the child He created us to be. If you are geared like I am, I want to get everything right. But the one thing I've learned to accept is that even though I'm wanting to get things right as I grow spiritually, it doesn't always work out that way. When I see my mistake, I need to accept it, and just like with my sewing, learn from it. Proverbs 24:16 says, "For the righteous man falls seven times, and rises again...." We need to move on from our mistakes and not get bogged down by them, even if it takes more than seven times to get it right. Everyone makes mistakes, so we don't need to sweat the small stuff. It's ok not to always get it right. Ok, for all of you perfectionists out there, you might have to read that line again ... it's OK not to always get it right.

We are so blessed to have the Bible that gives us clear instructions on how we are to live. But more than that, we are blessed that we serve a God who is gracious, and patient with us. He wants us to get things right more than we do, so if He's on our side ... sew on!!

43

Good morning! I was reading in Psalms this morning and I came across a verse that I've learned to really love. Psalm 139:14 says, "I will give thanks to Thee, for I am fearfully and wonderfully made." We are ALL uniquely made so no two people are alike. Many people think my younger sister and I are twins, which we are not. But even if we were twins, we would still not be exactly alike.

We serve such a creative God. For argument sake, let's just say that there are at least five billion people living on this earth. I have trouble sometimes just coming up with something different for dinner every night of the week, but not God. He came up with a unique combination for every single one of those five billion plus people He created. I don't know the number of possible combinations, but mathematically speaking, that's a lot of uniqueness going on.

The Lord is truly, truly amazing! Not only has He come up with all those different features and personalities, He intimately knows each of His creations, all the way down to the number of hairs on our head, as we're told in Matthew 10:30. "But the very hairs of your head are all numbered."

If God is creative enough to do all of that, is there any request that is too big for Him to handle? The answer to that question would be a resounding "NO!" So, here's to thanking God for all He is and for all He has created!

45...Being Guided

Good morning! I love technology, except when it is wrong. I recently had to find a friend's house in a city that I was only vaguely familiar with, so I was relying on the map app on my phone. I could tell as soon as I got into the town that the app was not giving me accurate directions. I had a decision to make. I could either blindly follow what the app was saying, or as Gibbs would say on NCIS, I could go with my gut. I'm not sure Gibbs' gut has ever let him down on the TV show. My choice was a toss-up but I went with my gut and turned off the map app on my phone and went with what made more sense. And thankfully, this time I got it right and was able to find my friend's house.

You know in life we have so many decisions to make on a daily basis and obviously we want to make the right decisions, so going with our gut might not always pan out. Do we have any other options? There are lots of things that try to help us as we are attempting to make good decisions. Just turn on the TV and watch the commercials. Most of them sound like whatever they are promoting is the only thing we need.

But I have a better place to go to get help. John 16:13 says, "But when He, the spirit of truth, comes, He will guide you into all the truth ..." The Holy Spirit lives within all Believers. He is incapable of steering us in the wrong direction. When we have the Holy Spirit living within us, we don't have to rely on anything else, not even our gut. So, here's to being guided by the only One that always gets it right!

46...Longing for a Loving Home

Good morning! I love the way God makes His word new to us. I've read this one verse in Proverbs before but today these words hit me as though they were brand-new. Proverbs 3:33 says, "The curse of the Lord is on the house of the wicked, but He blesses the dwelling of the righteous." You know how day by day we need to strive to be more like Christ, well, since the Lord has gone to Heaven and is building us a home, shouldn't our homes here reflect what our Heavenly homes will be like?

If so, what would those homes look like? I thought of a few things right off the bat. Our home should be ... a physically safe place, a place where words of encouragement are used often, a place that exhibits unconditional love, a place where there is tons of laughter, a place where hopes and dreams are nourished, a place where we can freely share our ideas, a safe place to ask questions, a place where we can try new things, a place where everything seems OK once we walk through the door ... and the list could go on and on.

I think I can sum up the list this way. Our earthly home should be a place we long to return to, just like we long for our home in Heaven. Since we are still a work in progress, I imagine all of our homes are also a work in progress. But the good news is that if our homes are not Heavenly examples, there is still time to fix that. So, here's to creating homes we and others want to come home to!

47...Everlasting Love

Good morning! We can learn a lot about love from our pets. I was thinking about that today as my sweet dog was showing me what unconditional love looks like. When I'm inside, Cope will sit on the front porch and look in the dining room window so he can see me. If I change rooms and go into the kitchen, he'll move to the front yard so he can see me through the kitchen window. And if it has been too long since he saw me through a window, he will start barking to get my attention. It is like he's telling me that he's always there, just inviting me to be with him and then he waits patiently for me to come out and play, even if it takes a while before that can happen.

This type of drawing love reminded me of the verse in Jeremiah 31:3 where the Lord says, "I have loved you with an everlasting love; therefore, I have drawn you with lovingkindness." The Lord is forever drawing us to Himself through His lovingkindness and He also waits patiently for us to come to Him. And just like with Cope, once I get outside to play with him, I wonder why I waited so long. God is patient with us as He waits for us to respond to Him. But I often wonder why time after time, I make Him wait at all because being with the Lord is the best place to be.

I don't know what is on your schedule today, but as it unfolds and you feel the Lord drawing you to Him, nothing could be more important to your day than taking the time to respond to His invitation. So, here's to being thankful for the Lord's everlasting love!

48...Flawless

Good morning! Recently, I printed off some pictures of my granddaughters. I wanted to enlarge the pictures to hang on the living room wall over the fireplace so I wanted them to be as perfect as I could get them. For each of the pictures I wanted to print, I was given the option to print them either in color or in black-and-white. I don't know why it is, but it seems like black-and-white pictures hide any and all imperfections.

On my way home from getting the pictures printed out, I heard a song by Mercy Me called "Flawless." This song gives us a black-and-white fact. It basically says that no matter what has happened in your life, once you ask the Lord to be the Lord of your life, by the Cross you are made flawless. Because our spotless Savior made the ultimate sacrifice on our behalf, God sees all Believers covered by the blood of Christ, making us flawless.

1 Peter 2:24 says, "and He Himself bore our sins in His body on the cross, that we might die to sin and live to righteousness; for by His wounds you were healed." If you want God to see you as flawless, all you have to do is put your trust and faith in Jesus. Now that the Lord has tied these two things together for me, the black-and-white pictures and the song, when I look at black-and-white pictures, I'll be thanking the Lord that my imperfections, my sins, have been covered. So, here's to being flawless!

49...Your Gift to God

Good morning! Don't you just love to see God at work? I sure do. Last week a girlfriend asked me to pray for her because her voice was as good as gone. It hurt to listen to her try to talk because it sounded like her throat was really hurting. Her weak voice had been with her for a couple of weeks already. Well, praise God, our prayers were answered and she got her voice back!

But what I really noticed was what she did with her voice once God returned it to her. She was helping lead the singing during worship time yesterday at church. She used that answered prayer to glorify God and to help us do the same by worshiping Him in song.

Her service to the Lord definitely reminded me of a quote from Leo Buscaglia. "Your talent is God's gift to you. What you do with it is your gift back to God." She gave her gift back to God and blessed us all in the process.

In Romans 12:6-8, we are told that in God's grace, He has given each of us different gifts and talents for doing certain things well. We all aren't singers but we do have a God-given talent. Our job is to determine what those gifts and talents are so we can then use them to serve Him. So, here's to a renewed desire to be obedient to God's call on each of our lives by using our talents and gifts to glorify Him and to serve others!

50...Our Guide

Good morning! It's good to be back home, sleeping in my own bed. They try to make you comfortable in the hospital, but as the old saying goes, "There's no place like home!" I have lots of time on my hands since I must be isolated for another eleven days, so I'm watching lots of different things on TV. Snow skiers caught my attention yesterday. It didn't take long to realize that I was watching blind skiers. No, they didn't have dogs with them, but they did have a guide. The relationship between the blind skier and his guide was one of total trust. The blind skier immediately followed the guide's instructions, knowing that the guide would get him safely down the mountain.

This relationship reminded me of the Scripture in Mark 4:9. "And He was saying, 'He who has ears to hear, let him hear.'" As Believers, the Holy Spirit is our guide down the mountain. Our relationship with Him also needs to be one of total trust. But too often we don't follow the blind skier's example. Could you imagine what would happen if the blind skier didn't obey the commands of his guide? The consequences of not obeying could be catastrophic. He could ski into a tree or even something worse.

Have you ever given any thought to what we miss out on or what we run into because we didn't immediately obey the voice of God? I want only God's best for my life and I know that listening to the Holy Spirit and trusting His commands immediately will get me there. Could I get there on my own? Maybe, but I also might run into a lot of things that I didn't have to. The choice is ours. So, here's to letting our guide, the Holy Spirit, bring us safely down life's mountain!

51...PRAISING GOD

Good morning! One thing I'm learning about grief is that you have absolutely no control over it, just like you had no control over the loss that you're grieving. I thought about this as I read Job 1:21. "...The Lord gave and the Lord has taken away. Blessed be the name of the Lord." I know that these verses were talking about Job's possessions but hang with me and I'll get to my point in a moment.

God gave permission to Satan to test Job but Job had the right attitude and the right motivation for serving the Lord. He understood that everything he had been given stewardship over actually belongs to God, and therefore he had no right to keep them. So when God needed to remove his possessions, Job understood that and went with God's flow of events. Whenever we see a tragedy like a hurricane, fire, tornado or an earthquake, when you talk to the survivors that have lost all their possessions, they typically say the same thing. "Things" can be replaced and they're just thankful their family was OK. Their statement agrees with Job's point of view.

So whether we are grieving over the loss of material possessions or people, the last part of verse 21 is the point that I've been learning. Even with all his loss, Job understood the importance of praising God. "Blessed be the name of the Lord." When we struggle with loss, the best way we can react is by praising the Lord and acknowledging His sovereignty. If we believe that God is in total control and our loss is just part of His plan for our life, making the choice to continue to worship and serve Him comes easier. Placing our trust in the Lord is a choice, but it's a choice worth making.

52...Swinging for the Fences

Good morning! With baseball's spring training in full swing, we know that spring weather isn't far behind. As I was thinking about all the things I'm looking forward to doing when the weather gets nicer, I was thrown a curve ball by a phone call. You see, someone that I love dearly isn't doing well physically. I already knew that part but the curve ball came when I heard the unexpected prognosis. I wasn't ready for that shock. Shortly after that news, a girlfriend sent me a sweet video of a 5-year-old boy finding out that he was going to get a new heart. The dad was telling his son that maybe they'd be able to go to a Red Sox's game this season after he got it, which thrilled the little boy. This video helped me put things in perspective.

Life and death are all part of our journey. We love when a new baby is born or when a young boy gets another shot at life by getting a new heart. It's the death part that always seems to throw us a curve. But for Christians, death means we are finally home with the Lord. 2 Corinthians 5:8 tells us that we should long for that eternal life and be of good courage and "prefer rather to be absent from the body and to be at home with the Lord."

Only the Lord knows when our appointed time is, and until that time, we need to live life with the same excitement and anticipation that five-year-old boy had about getting a new heart and we need to squeeze as much life out of our days and live them as though they were all home runs. So, here's to swinging for the fences!

53...THE SHORTEST DISTANCE

Good morning! It amazes me the things that we remember from our childhood. We hear something and it puts us back to the time when we were growing up. My sister gave me a plaque for my birthday last year that reminded me of a saying we heard as kids. The plaque states, "The shortest distance between two people is a smile." As kids, when we were grumpy or didn't get our way about something, we were often told to "turn that frown upside down." Do you remember that saying?

That was more than just a cute little saying, it actually was some really good advice. Proverbs 15:13 says, "A joyful heart makes a cheerful face." The smile then is the effect of a heart being joyful. I think that being thankful and joyful are like turkey and dressing. They just go together. As we start thanking God for all He's given us, a smile will naturally appear. A simple, sincere smile starts on the inside, but once it's shared, it can have a ripple effect as it is being shown to others. You can't be grumpy and smiling at the same time. Those two things just don't go together.

Have you ever noticed how people's smiles can bring light to a darkened room? A smile is something that is so easy to do and virtually everyone is physically capable of doing it. So as we go about our day, my prayer is that we let others see the joy in our hearts by the smiles on our faces. Here's to being thankful, joyful, and keeping the shortest distance between others!

54...An Intentional Life

Good morning! Do you live an intentional life? Living an intentional life means you purposely do things. Here are a couple of examples. When someone you love has a birthday, you intentionally go shopping to get them a card and maybe even a gift. You think of just them while you select the card and gift. Another example would be that when you go grocery shopping, you focus on what you and your family needs as you put items in your cart. You wouldn't be adding diapers and formula to your cart if you didn't have an infant to care for. So I think most people would answer my initial question with a "yes" response. I think it's easy for us to be purposeful with these examples.

Now let me ask a few more questions. Do you live an intentional life of faith? Do you intentionally set aside time for God? Do you purposely do Kingdom work? Do you intentionally put others before yourself? Psalm 105:4 says, "Seek the Lord and His strength; seek His face continually." If we keep our focus on the Lord and seek His face continually, it's much easier to live out an intentional life of faith.

Using Jesus as our example, the Bible is full of examples showing us how intentional He lived. God sent Him with a specific purpose in mind.

That purpose is found in John 3:16. "For God so loved the world, that He gave His only begotten Son, that whoever believes in Him should not perish, but have eternal life." Now that Jesus is back sitting at the right hand of the Father in Heaven, we have been given a part in God's plan. It is found in Matthew 28:19. "Go therefore and make disciples of all the nations ..." The New Testament is full of the ways we can intentionally further God's Kingdom. So, here's to finding out what they are and intentionally doing our part!

55...Imitators of Jesus

Good morning! We all know the old adage, "actions speak louder than words." I just saw that in action. A little boy, maybe seven- or eight-years-old, was walking with his dad across the parking lot to a local store. As a lady, aka … me, was also walking to the entrance of the store, the boy started running to the door as he hollered back to his dad, "I've got this one." By the time I got to the door, the little boy was standing there holding the door open for me. That father had obviously let his actions speak louder than words as he had taught his son how to be kind to others. It was all I could do not to pick up that little boy and give him a bear hug! As I looked back at the dad, the smile on my face must have conveyed my feelings. The dad said, "He's a good kid." My response to his comment was, "Because he has a good dad."

Raising children is a tough job but one well worth investing in. You don't have to be parents to influence how kids behave. As adults, we need to live out the way we want our children to become. Instead of just telling them what to do, we need to show them. They will do what they see us do, good or bad. Knowing that, we need them to see how we handle the situations that come across our path daily. Just like with this little boy, I am confident that he has seen his dad open the door for many ladies. By his actions, the dad showed his son how to be a gentleman. 1 Corinthians 11:1 reminds us that just like Paul, we need to be imitators of Jesus. "Be imitators of me, just as I am of Christ." We need to live out our life through the example that Jesus has shown us through His own actions. So, here's to giving the kids in our lives something worth imitating.

56...On Solid Ground

Good morning! With amazing help from friends, I'm in the process of making my backyard easier to maintain. It has a weird slant to it which creates perfect conditions for falling. As I've been working on figuring out the best way to handle this issue, I was reminded of the verse in Psalm 121:3. "He will not allow your foot to slip; He who keeps you will not slumber."

This verse is not talking about physically slipping like what I'm trying to prevent in my backyard. It's talking about how God has provided everything we need so that we can keep from sinning. His word gives us a path to walk on so we don't slip. Even though God has provided us with this smooth path to walk on, we are still sinners and so we will slip from time to time.

Unlike all of us, who have a limited amount of energy, God doesn't have to take time off to rest, which is why the second part of that verse brings me comfort. It says that God will not slumber. He is always there to give us a hand up when we fall, and until we get to Heaven, we will fall more times than we would care to. There are so many things in life that can cause us to fall but the good news is that the Lord will be there ready to pick us up, dust us off, and help us walk again on safe ground. So whatever is causing us to slip today, my prayer is that we would reach up and take God's hand. He wants to give us a solid footing!

57...Son-Shine

Good morning! We all experience trials in life. They come in all shapes, sizes, and severities. Thankfully, we don't have to go through any of the trials by ourselves. The Lord is always with us and He often gives us a human touch, too. I received several human touches yesterday in the forms of get-well cards, groceries, and an arrangement of Gerber daisies. The vase holding those beautiful flowers had a very familiar phrase on it. Live. Laugh. Love.

As I was looking at that phrase, I was reminded that's exactly what God wants us to do even, or especially, in the middle of trials. 1 Peter 5:10 says, "And after you have suffered for a little while, the God of all grace, who called you to His eternal glory in Christ, will Himself perfect, confirm, strengthen and establish you." No matter what trial you're going through, just remember, it will only last a short time compared the glorious eternal life we will one day live as Believers!

Showing kindness to those experiencing trials could be just the thing they need to help them get through the homestretch of their trial. My prayer is that we will always listen to the Holy Spirit and when He prompts us to do something kind for someone going through a hard time, that we will eagerly obey. The smallest acts of kindness can have huge impacts on someone suffering. So, here's to bringing Son-shine to another's cloudy days!

58...Marching Orders

Good morning! I think that it is natural to want to be the best at what we do. We want to get better at whatever it is, but I think too often in life we overlook the potential that we're already holding. We want to get all of our ducks in a row before we move to the next level. When God calls us to a task, we often hesitate because we don't think things are lined up correctly to do it.

I recently experienced that when God clearly told me that I was to host a Bible study with five beautiful ladies. He told me that even though we held a connection because we are all widows, He wanted us to build a stronger connection as being sisters in Christ. He had given me my marching orders ... feed them, love them, and learn from them. It took me a month to invite them and two more weeks before we started. Now that we've completed the Bible study, I can't imagine why I waited so long to do what I was told, especially since one of the ladies had her cancer return and has now passed away. I am thankful that we were able to share that time together. I would have missed out on so much if I would have not been obedient to what God called me to do.

1 Peter 4:10 says, "As each one has received a special gift, employ it in serving one another, as good stewards of the manifold grace of God." The moral of this story is that we should use our God-given gifts and talents to help change the world we live in, whether it be with 1, 5 or 500. So, here's to serving God with the gifts He's already given us!

59...Search Me

Good morning! Hunting season is in full swing. But before the season starts, hunters spend lots of time getting ready for opening day. There are stands to work on and other equipment to get ready. Hunters are passionate about their sport. They get out before the first light and might not come back until way after sunset. Hunters wait patiently in the woods, hoping to see and take down that perfect trophy.

We all know that hunters search the woods as they hunt, but did you know that it's good to let the Lord search us? Psalm 139:23-24 says, "Search me, O God, and know my heart; try me and know my anxious thoughts; and see if there be any hurtful way in me, and lead me in the way everlasting." Just as we know that there are deer in the woods, we can be sure that there are things not pleasing to the Father within all of us. Some of those things we may already know about, but others things might be unnoticed by us. They may be things like wrong motives for wanting something done, trying to control things that are not for us to control, jealousy over what others have and we don't, or unchecked anger that is just waiting to erupt.

We need to ask God to bring light to all those hidden things so we can deal with them. It's often those things that we don't recognize that cause us the most harm. But exposing them to the Light is the best way to handle them. We won't be that "perfect trophy" until we are in Heaven, but until then, here's to a productive search!

60...BLESSED

Good morning! One year ago today, Alan entered Heaven. I know that I speak for many when I say, "I miss that man!" One of the lessons I'm learning through his loss is that keeping the proper perspective is what helps me to get through the days without him.

James 4:14 says that our lives here are just a vapor that appears for a little while and then vanishes away. Although it seems like we've already lived so long without Alan, much more than a vapor, when we look at this year from God's perspective, it truly is just a mist compared to eternity.

Today, I want to thank the Lord for two things. First, that each of us have the same opportunity to go from this vapor of time into eternity in Heaven, just like Alan did. It is that hope we have through Jesus that helps us put one foot in front of the other as we keep on living.

And secondly, I say, "Thank you Lord for all the help You have provided me through the love of family and friends." Because I know his passing was the best for Alan, though some days I still swim through a pool of tears, my prayer is for the Lord to help me daily say, and mean it, "it is well, with my soul." So thank you for your prayers, love and support, not only for me, but for the entire family. God continues to abundantly bless us as we go through this healing process!

61...Safe Passage

Good morning! We all experience change in our lives but there's a big difference in the types of changes we face. Some changes might be minimal things like you can't go to lunch until 12:30 instead of noon. OK, sure that's a change but it doesn't rock your boat, or at least it shouldn't. So what do you do you when life-altering changes happen and you feel like the boat you're in is about to capsize? Where do you turn for safe passage through these waves of change?

In the nautical world, light houses are used to guide you so that your boat doesn't end up in areas that would be harmful. When you feel like your boat is trying to sink from major changes, make sure that you have the right light to guide you safely through. Jesus is our Light. The good news is that we can be like David and be confident that the Lord is always with us. Psalm 16:8 says, "I have set the Lord continually before me; because He is at my right hand, I will not be shaken."

Just like steering boats through rough waters, if we keep our focus on the Light, Jesus, we will safely get to where He is taking us, regardless of how big the waves are that we are dealing with. It's true that we might not like the ride of change in our life, and even though we didn't have a say in the matter, we have to just trust that the Lord knows best. So, when big changes come in our life, here's to keeping our boats upright by following Jesus!

62...Reputations Worth Having

Good morning! Last night I was reading in the book of Acts. I stopped on a verse that really got me thinking. Acts 10:22 says, "… Cornelius, a centurion, a righteous and God-fearing man well-spoken of by the entire nation of the Jews …" This verse was talking about how this man's reputation had preceded him, in a good way. I think it's important that we consider our own reputation. What kind of reputation are we building by the way we are living our lives? When our name is mentioned, how do people respond to it? Hopefully people respond in a positive manner like Cornelius. His character had obviously helped him create a good reputation among others.

Your words and actions matter. Social media has its good points but one of its downfalls is that some people hide behind a screen. They say things to others and about others that they wouldn't say face to face to someone. But if you have built a good reputation, even when people try to malign you, those that hear the accusations won't believe it and the one speaking those lies will make themselves look like a fool.

The beautiful thing about people that have a good reputation is that they never have to respond to negative allegations. They can just stay quiet and let their character speak for itself. So, here's to being like Cornelius, one who fears God and has established a good reputation!

63...Preventing Tragedy

Good morning! Do you ever have one of those "lightbulb" moments? You know, when something pops in your head and all of a sudden you understand what's going on, as though someone had just shed some light on the matter. I had one as I was reading in the book of Matthew. In Chapter 5 verse 45, it tells us that God "causes His sun to rise on the evil and the good, and sends rain on the righteous and the unrighteous." While we are here on earth, everyone, good and evil, gets to enjoy **some** of God's blessings.

Maybe that's why so many people don't think they need God in their lives. They live day to day under the assumption that they are in charge and are doing just fine on their own. They probably don't give much thought to what happens after they die. And if they do, they might think because they were in charge here on earth that they can also be in charge of their eternal destiny, which is actually true, but not in the way they would be thinking.

That's why it is so important for Christians to witness to those who are living their lives apart from the Lord. They need to understand that if they separate themselves from God in this life, then after death, they will still be separated from God for all eternity. So here's to helping others prevent the tragedy of spending eternity away from God. It's the ultimate gift of love you can show them. I am thankful someone showed me!

64...Seeking Shelter

Good morning! We have been blessed with a couple of fantastic weather days. The sun is shining, which has helped people's mood, and everything looks a bit brighter with so much light. We can all agree that these kind of days are good but what about the days when it's storming and the sun is not shining, leaving everything dark and dreary? Figuratively speaking, when storms or trials come into our lives, do we see them as something terrible or as a potentially good thing?

It goes against the flesh to think that there could be something good come out of something terrible but I've experienced enough storms to know that what at first seems like something really bad can turn out to be a blessing. When you are in the middle of these storms, I know it is often hard to see anything positive happening. There's just a lot of thunder and lightning between points A and Z.

Even though God allows these hardships, they are never meant to hurt us. Jeremiah 29:11 tells us that God's plans for us are "for welfare and not for calamity." Could it be possible that God is disrupting our plans so He can implement His? When you think of storms like that, it's kind of hard to be disgruntled about them because God always knows what's best for us and if He says an interruption is necessary, then so be it. So when your storm hits, here's to finding protection under God's umbrella. It's always open to those that seek it.

65...New Beginnings

Good morning! There are many times in our lives when we start over. It might be because we get married, or divorced. It could be that we moved, not just across town, but to a new city or state. Maybe we make a career change, doing something that we've never done before. Even though new beginnings can be awesome, we often fear these new starts. But if you think about it, every single day is a new start. Each day is a new beginning. Daily, we are given a new chance to make a difference in life.

Lamentations 3:22-23 says, "The Lord's lovingkindnesses indeed never cease, for His compassions never fail. They are new every morning; great is Thy faithfulness." Great is His faithfulness! So then why does the fear factor come into play as we start over? I think it's because of the unknown. We like things nice, neat and orderly and we would like to know how things are going to roll out in our new beginnings. Will I like where I've moved to? Will the new career and I get along?

There's a reason why God tells us to only focus on today. It takes faith to live day by day, allowing God to lead and orchestrate the events in our life and I don't think our limited minds could even handle more than just the information for today. But what a fun and exciting ride it can be when we let God lead it. So, here's to embracing new beginnings and anticipating all the good that God has in store for us through these new starts!

66...Finish Well

Good morning! Last week while working outside, I was stung by a wasp. It's amazing how something that little can hurt so much. This morning as I was taking another look at it with a magnifying glass to make sure I didn't have any stinger still left in there, I began thinking about Paul and the story of the thorn in his side.

2 Corinthians 12 tells us about this well-known story. Paul looked at that thorn as something from the enemy that the Lord had allowed with the purpose of keeping Paul humble. Paul prayed three times that the thorn might leave him. The answer was always no, so the thorn continued. I'm not sure if this "thorn" was a physical problem or maybe it was a person that was bringing Paul a lot of grief. Paul talks about a person causing him real pain in 2 Timothy 4:14. "Alexander the coppersmith did me much harm; the Lord will repay him according to his deeds."

The Lord doesn't take it well when others cause His children pain. Regardless of this pain that Paul was experiencing, he never left the path that God had put him on. Paul fought the good fight and finished well by keeping the faith. In other words, he stayed strong for the Lord and in the Lord. My prayer is that we can learn from Paul's example. Whatever the "thorn" is in your side, keep your focus on the Lord and He will help you finish well!

67...Good Conscience

Good morning! Do you have smoke detectors in your house? If you're like me, you have more than one. My sleep was disrupted last night with an obnoxious beep, beep, beep…. I kept asking myself, "What is that noise?" As important as these detectors are, 3:00 in the morning is no time to try to figure out which smoke alarm is making that annoying sound because the batteries needed to be changed.

God gives us ways to detect problems, too. It's our conscience. 1 Timothy 1:18-19 says, "This command I entrust to you, Timothy, my son, in accordance with the prophecies previously made concerning you, that by them you may fight the good fight, keeping faith and a good conscience, which some have rejected and suffered shipwreck in regard to their faith." The conscience has a great value for Christians. It detects when we start moving outside of the Lord's standards and sends out a warning. The Holy Spirit uses that signal to get our attention. He will then reveal what the problem is just like the noise a smoke detector makes to warn us of danger. But thankfully, He does more than that. He gives us an understanding of the problem, and shows us the right choices to make. He will guide us to relevant Bible verses that can shed light on our situation and point out the consequences of making a wrong choice.

Just like batteries are needed to keep my smoke detectors working correctly, reading God's Word is necessary in order to keep a good conscience. Here's to yielding to God's warnings and avoiding those bad choices!

68...More Strength, Please

Good morning! So what do you do when others try to make your life miserable? How do you respond? When you just read that initial question, what person or persons popped up in your head? Is it that person that sits next to you at work? Is it a neighbor, someone at church, or maybe someone close to you? Do you lay awake at night and try to figure out why they're like this? Let me help you get some more sleep. Instead of losing sleep over them, the best thing we can do is to ask God for extra strength. No, that's not extra physical strength so we can wring their little necks, which is what our flesh wants to do, but it's that strength needed not to retaliate and to help us do our best to show God's love and grace to that individual.

Plain and simple, why this happens is because we live in a fallen world and the enemy enjoys using people to shake us up, even those closest to us. It even happened to Jesus. Matthew 26:14–16 tells of the account of Judas, one of the original twelve disciples. Judas is known for his betrayal of Jesus. He betrayed Jesus for only thirty silver coins. This started the chain of events that led to the crucifixion of our Lord.

Our issues in no way compare to the intensity of this example of Jesus but hopefully it will help us the next time someone tries to yank our chain. Just remember that we have a Lord who understands. Take a deep breath, give yourself a moment or two to get the right perspective on the situation, and ask God for the extra strength you need because this too shall pass. God gave the strength that Jesus needed and thankfully, He will give it to us, too!

69…A New Look

Good morning! Alan was a master at repurposing. I think he would be tickled at how I'm doing that now, too. Take my fire pit area for example. That area used to be a covered dog pen. The dog pen has been taken down but the concrete block floor remained, which was perfect to put the fire pit on. The tin that was on the roof of the dog pen was used to make some needed repairs on Alan's shop. And still other pieces of the wood from the pen was used to replace worn out boards on the two benches I've put in the pit area. Repurposing … gotta love it!

That difference between reusing the old or replacing with the new reminded me of what it means to be saved through Jesus. In John 3:3, Jesus says, "Truly, truly, I say to you, unless one is born again, he cannot see the kingdom of God." Being saved, or born again, means that you have a new life in Christ. He doesn't just renovate your existing life; He replaces it with a new one. And the new life begins by asking the Lord to live in your heart.

Just like with my benches, you will notice a huge change when that happens. Your life will become strong in Jesus, like my benches did with new 2x4's. I'm so glad that through God's Word, He makes it crystal clear how to become a child of God by being born again. Those who have seen my benches say they look brand new, so here's to praying others can see that your life looks new too, once you've been saved!

70...Its Proper Place

Good morning! We've all heard the saying, "There's a place for everything and everything has its place." It's amazing, but even after decades have passed, I can still remember things my parents taught me growing up. As I've been doing projects around the house, I've been reminded of a simple tool I got from my parents. That tool, or lesson, was to only handle things one time. So when you use something, it immediately needs to be put back in its proper place. That way, you only handle it once.

I wish that with my sins, I would only have to deal with them once and then put them where they belong, alongside all my other forgiven sins in that sin-graveyard. But too often, I repeat the same sin. I wish I would only have to be convicted about them once and never repeat them again. But since that doesn't happen, I'm very thankful that we have a God who forgives our sins each and every time we commit them when we repent.

One of Satan's tactics is to convince us that when we commit a sin more than once, God really doesn't forgive us. The enemy would love nothing more than for us to wallow in the guilt of our sins. But Psalm 103:12 tells us that not only does God forgive our sins but He wipes them completely from His presence. If God doesn't hang on to our past sins, we shouldn't either. So, here's to putting everything, including our sins, in its proper place!

71...Believing

Good morning! Sports really can mirror life. Take baseball for example. On a regular basis, as a St. Louis Cardinal fan, I'll see Yadier Molina, the catcher, go out to the mound to calm the pitcher down and encourage him to focus on just this one batter. There's just something about focusing on the here and now. I think it comes down to this question, "Do you believe?" In baseball, unless the pitcher has the belief that he can get this batter out, chances are that he won't.

Let's take that "Do you believe?" question and apply it to something much more important in life. Scripture also tells us to focus on the here and now. Matthew 6:34 says, "Therefore do not be anxious for tomorrow; for tomorrow will take care of itself. Each day has enough trouble of its own." God tells us to stay focused on what's in front of us, just looking at today. In order to do that, we must say "yes" to the question, "Do you believe?" Do you believe that we serve a God who is bigger than any obstacle or any problem that could come our way? Do you believe that God is who He says He is and that He has our best interest at heart? Do you believe that He will keep every single promise that He has made?

Just like the pitcher, unless we can answer "yes" to those questions, we won't be throwing strikes. God has a game plan for each of us but if we don't believe that He is capable of orchestrating our life for our good and His glory, we won't be any more successful than a pitcher on the mound that doesn't believe that the catcher is calling for the right pitch. Life can certainly throw us a lot of curveballs, but if we believe that God can handle any pitch that comes our way, then we're well on our way to having a winning record in life. Here's to believing in the One who can.

72...Being Equipped

Good morning! Have you ever noticed when it comes to doing jobs around the house that we often spend as much time working on our equipment as we do actually using it? I'm learning that there comes a time when we just have to wave our white flag and ask for help. I recently bought a corded weed eater. It only weighs 5 pounds so it's something that I can easily use.

But the problem with the weed eater is that at some point, you are going to run out of string. I tried and tried, and tried some more, to get new string put back in it with no luck. So after about an hour of this battle, I swallowed my pride and took the weed eater up to the local hardware store. The gentleman that helped me was able to show me what I was doing wrong in about two minutes. So I was back home and ready to continue weed eating in about a 15-minute span. And the next time I run out of string, I will know how to put new string in it.

I am so thankful that when God calls us to a job, He also equips us. Hebrews 13:21 tells us that He will "equip you in every good thing to do His will, working in us that which is pleasing in His sight, through Jesus Christ, to whom be the glory forever and ever. Amen." God gives us every single thing that we need to do the task He puts before us. The only thing we must do is to say, "Yes, Lord." So, here's to surrendering to the jobs God has for us … no equipment necessary!

73...It Takes Three

Good morning! I recently attended a very sweet wedding. God was truly at the heart of this ceremony. The couple illustrated Ecclesiastes 4:9-12. These verses talk about how it's better to have a partner and friend who can be there to help, warm, and protect. Verse 12 says, "And if one can overpower him who is alone, two can resist him. A cord of three strands is not quickly torn apart." For this couple, the three strands represented the bride, the groom and the Lord. They had a wooden cross with the three strands secured on the top of the cross. Together, as the music played, they braided the strands to make one thick cord which couldn't be easily broken.

That is the perfect illustration for a successful marriage. A marriage takes three to be complete. This couple is grounded enough in their faith to understand that God needs to be the center of their marriage. We live in a fallen world so people are going to falter and divorces will happen.

With that being said, I believe the best advice we could give newlyweds is to explain to them that if each looked to the Lord to complete them, and not each other, then their spouse would just be the icing on the cake. By doing this, they will have developed a pattern of running to God when problems arise and praising God for all His blessings individually and as a couple. For me, the most beautiful part of this wedding was that this sweet couple chose to put God front and center, just as He will be in their marriage. So, here's to celebrating the love that God has joined together!

74...Clearly Shown

Good morning! There are things that I don't know how to do around my place. When one of those things arise, I always say that would be an "Alan question." Obviously, I can't ask Alan anymore, but fortunately there are plenty of people willing to help. I had a slow water leak going on but I couldn't find the source of it, so every month my water bill was going up. When I got things outside ready for the winter and brought in my hoses, one of my outside spickets wouldn't shut off all the way. I thought I had found the leak.

To make a long story short, when the repair guys showed up, we were having trouble finding my main water shut off. We were able to find the outside shut off but not the main one so I called the water company and they said they'd send someone out to show me. And they did. When we went back to try to find the blue flag they left, I had to laugh. Not only did they flag the spot in the woods, they also drew a big, blue arrow on the lane so we couldn't miss it. ☺

Doesn't God have to do the same thing with us sometimes? We wander around lost, not finding what we need and often just end up going around in circles. But the good news is that God has given us a big, blue arrow, too, to be our compass in life … the Bible. As Psalm 37:23 tells us, "The steps of a man are established by the Lord …" If God then is showing us the way we should go in life, we must stay in His word to get the directions for the path He wants us to follow. So today, I'm thankful for the clarity He gives us, like big, blue arrows and His word!

75...Walk On

Good morning! During sandal-wearing weather, lots of ladies go to their favorite salon to get a pedicure. We just love pretty toes, but do you know who loves our feet? God does! I had to chuckle when I read this in Isaiah 52:8, since I just got a pedicure. "How lovely on the mountains are the feet of him [her] who brings good news, who announces peace and brings good news of happiness, who announces salvation, and says to Zion, 'Your God reigns!'"

Our feet carry us to wherever we go. We might not climb a mountain to bring the good news of Jesus but I think it would be cool to climb to the top of a mountain and proclaim with arms outstretched that our God reigns! What we can do is let our feet take us to the hospital or nursing home to visit a friend, just to remind them that they are loved and definitely not alone. Those same feet can take us lots of places to do other tasks that the Lord lays on our hearts.

Sometimes our feet are tired and we put off doing what the Holy Spirit is prompting us to do. I know I'm guilty of that but once I realize that my feet have gotten lazy, I brush them off and start stepping out once again to be a messenger of God's love and promises to those who need Him. The blessings that come from God when we're stepping out in the right direction feel much better than any pedicure. ☺ So here's to walking in service to the Lord!

76...Living in an A+ World

Good morning! My car insurance company gives you an option to lower your premiums by allowing them to monitor your driving. They sent me a little gadget that I plugged in my car under the dash. When I start the car, it'll beep three times to let me know it's working and to remind me to drive safely. I received my first report card. It said I was a B+ driver because on a few occasions, I apparently hit the brakes too hard. Ok, the way I'm wired, anything less than an "A" won't cut it.

It is so easy to get wrapped up in circumstances of life. When things go crazy in our lives, we often try to fix the craziness ourselves. These attempts are usually exhausting and often unproductive. What we should do instead is put the brakes on, as hard as you'd like, and turn to Jesus.

Philippians 4:6-7 says, "Be anxious for nothing, but in everything by prayer and supplication with thanksgiving let your request be made known to God. And the peace of God, which surpasses all comprehension, shall guard your hearts and your minds in Christ Jesus." God wants us to take all our craziness to Him. He is the One who can turn things around for us. He sees the bigger picture and will use the challenging situations in life for His glory and our good, if we let Him. The good, the bad and the less than an "A" world is all around us. But thankfully, the good news is that we can live in the A+ world of Jesus!

77...REAL HOPE

Good morning! For many years now, part of my morning routine has been getting a call from my younger sister. (No, to the surprise of many, we are not twins but we've been asked that for too many years to count.) Anyway, the other morning we were trying to have our typical conversation but we were both yawning so much it was hard to talk. I suggested she get a cup of coffee and she said that coffee was just a false hope. You just can't replace the real thing and in this case the real thing for us was more sleep.

But don't we do that in life? We try to replace what we really need with something else and then are surprised when it doesn't work. The only hopes that don't disappoint are those that come from the Lord, like the hope of salvation found in John 3:16. "For God so loved the world, that He gave His only begotten Son, that whoever believes in Him should not perish, but have eternal life." And the hope given to us in Psalm 48:14 says that God is our constant companion and our guide through this life. The hope of rest is found in Matthew 11:28. "Come to me, all who are weary and heavy-laden, and I will give you rest."

These are just a few of the many hopes we have through our Lord. God's word is filled with hopes meant to encourage us. So if you know someone today who is just pooped because of what life is dishing out, take the time to encourage them with the hope found in Jesus Christ. A simple text or phone call could mean the world to them. I know it did for me.

78...With Heart

Good morning! I received a sweet card from friends of mine that had this quote from Helen Keller on it. "The best and most beautiful things in the world cannot be seen or even touched, they must be felt with the heart." I have thought about that quote often since reading it and the last part of it is what keeps speaking to me. The most beautiful things must be felt with the heart. When you think about it, her quote is absolutely right. What is the last thing that brought you to tears? It was something that tugged at your heart, right?

As I was answering that question for myself, I had a "duh" moment. 1 Corinthians 3:16 says, "Do you not know that you are a temple of God, and that the Spirit of God dwells in you?" When we receive Christ as our Lord and Savior, the Holy Spirit immediately moves into our heart. So of course, the most beautiful things in life have to be felt with the heart because that's where Christ is.

I wonder if Ms. Keller was thinking about that spiritual truth when she spoke those words or if she was just referring to her lack of sight. Either way, her words ring true. If you want to experience the most beautiful things in life, then you have to invite Jesus into your heart. If you haven't already done so, then today would be a perfect day to start experiencing life's best through faith in Jesus Christ. He's waiting to move in as soon as you give Him the green light to do so!

79...Starting the Day Right

Good morning! As you've started another day, have you talked with God yet? The simply act of saying good morning to the Lord and asking Him to help you navigate through this day takes only a few seconds but this acknowledgement will put your day on the right track.

I recently heard someone say that they do not pray much because they do not want to pray something that is not part of God's will. At the time, I couldn't remember the Scripture to challenge their statement. And I knew that trying to explain, with my own argument, how that wasn't possible would not have been enough to convince them. They needed that proof. So here's the proof from God's word. Romans 8:26-27 says,

> *And in the same way the Spirit also helps our weaknesses; for we do not know how to pray as we should, but the Spirit Himself intercedes for us with groanings too deep for words; and He who searches the hearts knows what the mind of the Spirit is, because He intercedes for the saints according to the will of God.*

So you see, there's no reason to worry about not praying for the right things. The Lord takes our prayers and intercedes for us, only taking those things to God that are in His will for us. Knowing this, frees us up to pray all day long. As we go through this day, we can talk to God about everything ... what we see and hear, the needs of others and ourselves, and thanking Him for all the blessings of this day. Praying is one of the greatest privileges we have. As Christians, we are never alone because the Lord is always with us and ready to talk. Praying is the best way to start a Monday, as well as a Tuesday, Wednesday, Thursday, Friday, Saturday, and Sunday!

80...Eastern Sky

Good morning! I have been thinking a lot about how cool the total solar eclipse was. There are some really amazing pictures of it being posted online. But what I keep thinking about the most is all the hype that led up to the day we saw the total solar eclipse. People traveled many, many miles just so that they were here to be able to see it. A friend told me that a friend of hers came all the way from Japan to see it. Our local television station did an eclipse 2017 countdown. It was on the national news and it was the topic of conversation for quite a while before that historical day.

When the total eclipse actually happened, people were cheering and some were crying over how awesome the event was. Can you imagine what this world would be like if all Christians were waiting with that same anticipation for the return of Jesus? Maybe that enthusiasm isn't there because we don't know exactly when that will be. Matthew 24:36 says, "But of that day and hour no one knows, not even the angels of Heaven, nor the Son, but the Father alone." But just because we can't have a countdown to His return, we still need to live our days like Jesus was returning today.

As cool as the eclipse was, Joel 2:31-32 tells us that a more impressive event is going to happen. "The sun will be turned into darkness, and the moon into blood, before the great and awesome day of the Lord comes." When the Lord returns, everyone on earth will be able to see Him, not just those in a specific path like the eclipse was. So, until that day, may our eyes be focused on the Eastern sky as we wait with great anticipation for the return of Jesus.

81...Reminders

Good morning! As we go through our day, there are literally hundreds of requests we could take to the Lord in prayer. I don't have any trouble remembering to pray for the most heartbreaking things, like my girlfriend's husband who just had a terrible accident and now has a long road of recovery ahead of him. I don't know about you but sometimes I need a reminder to pray for those things that aren't as horrific.

On the way to town, there's a billboard that has a picture of my heart doctor, his nurse and staff on it. And every time I pass it, I take a moment to thank God for the skills that He has given my cardiologist and his team as they take care of not only me but all their patients. God has given me a better quality of life as a result of their God-given skills. I also ask the Lord to bless their families because they often sacrifice time with them so they can take care of patients like me.

Prayer is absolutely essential to our Christian walk. It not only allows us to bring requests before the Lord but it's a time to thank God for who He is and what He has done. Scripture tells us in 1 Thessalonians 5:17-18 to "pray without ceasing; in everything give thanks; for this is God's will for you in Christ Jesus." Throughout the day, the Lord wants us to talk to Him about everything we experience. These typically aren't long prayers but a short acknowledgment of the blessings He is providing and the things that we encounter that need some divine intervention. Praying this way is just like talking to a good friend who we get the privilege to hang out with all day long. Prayer reminders come in all sorts of ways, not just billboards. So, here's to using those reminders to initiate another conversation with our Lord.

82...Rain in Our Hearts

Good morning! I hope you've noticed the benefits of our much needed rain showers. At my house, the plants have already started looking a little livelier after the rain. But what I have noticed most is that the leaves on the trees that had curled inward, as though they were totally drying up, have once again stretched out their leaves, preparing to receive any moisture they could get.

As I was watching things spring back to life, Isaiah 58:11 came to mind. "The Lord will guide you always; He will satisfy your needs in a sun-scorched land and will strengthen your frame. You will be like a well-watered garden; like a spring whose waters never fail." We are so much like the leaves on the trees. When we don't get what's necessary to sustain us, we also start withering.

When the obstacles of life cause us to recoil, we start pulling inward, trying to shield ourselves. But that's absolutely opposite of what we need to do. When we feel ourselves lacking, that's exactly when we need to stretch out our hands and receive God's promises. Those promises are the living water we receive through God's word. He left us His words so we would know how to survive seasons of drought and seasons of plenty. So, here's to having a strong frame by letting the Holy Spirit rain in our hearts through God's words, and giving us everything we need to sustain us, especially during dry spells.

83...Don't Be Late

Good morning! As a new school year is getting ready to start, I'm sure there are some anxious kids out there. When I was in school, I remember being the most concerned about being late for class. Because I knew if I was late, then there was usually a price to pay for my tardiness. I so appreciated the teachers who understood that when there were literally a hundred girls trying to use the bathroom between classes, sometimes you'd just be late. I think the rule then was if you were reported late three times, you'd have to serve a detention. So, there were consequences, but they were minimal.

However, there is a time in our life that being late will have massive, eternal consequences. If you are late in making a decision for Christ and die before you give your life to Him, then there isn't anything that can be done at that point to make up for your tardiness. Scripture tells us in Mark 16:16 that those who believe will be saved and those that don't believe will be condemned.

The decision whether or not to ask Jesus to be your Lord and Savior is a decision that everyone has to make for themselves. There would be no better way to start a new school year than going into it knowing you've already made the most important decision of your life, asking Jesus into your heart. Everything else would be a piece of cake. So, here's to praying that students, teachers, administration, support staff and parents will enter this school year being guided and directed by the ultimate teacher, Jesus Christ.

84...He's Always There

Good morning! As I was talking with a friend who was going through a significant problem, she questioned where God was in the middle of her circumstances. Have you ever asked God, "Where are You?" as you're going through a crisis? I think we all have.

I wish I could have a do-over with my answer to my friend. I found the perfect answer in Psalm 68:19. "Blessed be the Lord, who daily bears our burdens, the God who is our salvation." The answer to her question is that He is right here, wanting to carry our burdens. He's just waiting for us to hand our problems over to Him, so He can do what He does best ... take care of EVERYTHING!

We don't just want to have a "crisis-relationship" with the Lord. This verse tells us He wants to bear our daily burdens. In order to do that, we need to do our part and be in daily communication with Him ... praying. He wants to be involved in every detail of our day.

Once we get in the mindset and habit of talking to the Lord about everything, when a crisis comes, we won't have to wonder where He is. We will know that He is right here with us, just like He is with everything else that shows up in our day. So, here's to building that strong, daily-relationship with the Lord!

85...Keep It Simple

Good morning! Does praying ever just wear you out emotionally, as well as spiritually? We will get back to this question in a minute. Have you noticed how God can say so much with only a few words? Me, not so much ... LOL ☺ I was looking over some of my prayers that I have written down to try to figure out why it takes me so many words, and then it hit me.

I guess I forgot that since God is fully aware of everything that is happening, I really don't have to give Him a recap of events. I also don't have to give him a commentary on the issues based on how I feel about them. And I sure don't need to be giving the Lord possible answers to my request.

Matthew 11:29 tells us that we are supposed to learn from God. So, since God uses fewer words, that's what I want to do, too. I'm thinking the fewer the words, the better the prayer. All of the elaboration that I do in my prayers isn't necessary. I just need to bring the request to Him and let Him be God. I need to talk less and listen more when it comes to my prayer life.

Sometimes prayers just need to be as short and simple as three words ..."Lord, help me!" Since God is definitely clued in to what's happening here and what's going on in everyone's lives, here's to keeping our prayers simple!

86...God's Appointments

Good morning! "Random acts of kindness" were really talked about a couple years ago. The news media made a big deal over them, as though this was some sort of new concept. But God's word teaches us that if we have the power to act, we are to be about those random acts of kindness in our everyday life.

Proverbs 3:27 says, "Do not withhold good from those to whom it is due, when it is in your power to do it." And in the next verse, verse 28, the Lord calls us not to put off doing good until a later time. He sets up these "random acts of kindness" appointments just for us to fulfill. These appointments might be something you do for your family, someone at work, an acquaintance, or a total stranger. Our job is to be tuned in to the Lord so we're not late for these appointments or miss them all together. So often we are looking and waiting to help with the big things, but I think the little, practical things are some of the best appointments given. Think of the last time you did something nice for someone. Was it a big or little thing you did? I bet it was something little and I bet it put a big smile on someone's face.

If you go through a day without doing something kind for someone else, I wouldn't call that much of a day at all. As Christians, showing the Lord's kindness to others should be something that comes as natural as breathing. So, here's to looking for and acting on the appointments God has set up for us!

87...Healing Our Wounds

Good morning! Do you have any wounds? They may be from a surgery or an injury. When we have them, normally we have gone to someone else to help heal them, like a doctor. These people have been trained to help you get better. But what about those wounds that nobody but God sees? What do you do with those spiritual or emotional wounds of the heart? Maybe you've prayed for years about something but haven't gotten the answer you've longed for and you wonder why God isn't giving you what you've requested. Or maybe it's a loss that has rocked your world causing you deep pain and you just don't understand why this happened.

When dealing with those wounds, we need to be reminded of a couple of things. First of all, God is a great healer and He wants to take all of those wounds away from us. He understands. He experienced the greatest spiritual and emotional wounds ever when He died on the cross for us. Secondly, we have to remember that God has planned out our life, knowing in advance what the chapters of our life will look like. And lastly, we have to trust that He will take all our wounds and turn them around for our good. That's where our faith comes in.

So the question we need to answer is whether we believe that God is able to ... deal with our wounds, understand our pain, and bring good out of our deepest hurts. Psalm 34:18 tells us that the Lord is close to the brokenhearted and saves those who are crushed in spirit. And Jeremiah 29:11 reminds us that the Lord's plans are to prosper us and not to harm us. His plans are to give us hope and a future. All we need to do is turn those wounds over to God and let Him heal us from the inside out.

88...It Gets Even Better

Good morning! As I was enjoying being out on my swing this morning, I was looking around with great anticipation and envisioning what my backyard would look like when all the new grass comes up. I liked the picture I saw in my head.

You know, the older I get, the more I anticipate and like the picture I see of Heaven in my head. One of the things I am really looking forward to is being reunited with loved ones that have entered Heaven before me. Paul asks in 1 Thessalonians 2:19, "For who is our hope or joy or crown of exultation? Is it not even you, in the presence of our Lord Jesus and His coming?" Paul is telling us by that question that Christians who he loved on earth will be his joy in Heaven. But it gets even better than that.

As good as our relationships were with those loved ones on earth, they will be "perfect" relationships in Heaven. There will be no fighting, no jealousy, no unkind words ... you get the idea. Can you just imagine what a day would be like when every person you encountered would love you "perfectly" just like Jesus does? When I envision that, it just blows my mind. I can't wait to experience that!

So, the next time someone is unkind to you, just chuckle to yourself as you remember that once they get to Heaven, they won't be like that. They will totally be the person that God created them to be, and therefore, nothing unkind can come from them. It makes it much easier to "turn the other cheek."

89...Listen to Me

Good morning! Have you ever noticed how kids will repeat what they've been told or heard at the most inopportune times? I recently witnessed such a situation. I was waiting for a mom and what proved to be a sassy, little boy to move away from the door so I could go inside the post office. The mom was on her cell phone and her son was wanting her attention. He tugged at the bottom of her shirt, which didn't get the attention from her that he was wanting. So he tugged a little more, and still no response from his mom. And then when his gentle calls of "Mom!" didn't work, he put his hands on his hips and yelled, "Put that phone down and listen to me!" Well, that got her attention, and everyone else's, too. He'd obviously heard that a time or two himself!

This reminded me of what God had to say in Matthew 17:5, "While he was still speaking, behold, a bright cloud overshadowed them, and behold, a voice out of the cloud, saying, 'This is My beloved Son, with whom I am well-pleased; listen to Him!'" I'm not sure if God had His hands on His hips or not, but He sure got everyone's attention.

I don't know about you, but if the Creator of Heaven and earth says in His word that we are to be listening to His Son, then I'm going to be listening to Jesus. And more than that, I'm going to be repeating what He says, every chance I get, just not with my hands on my hip. So, here's to keeping our ears open!

90...Praise Him

Good morning! Have you ever been in a situation that almost literally took the breath out of you? It's those times that we become figuratively frozen. We just can't seem to move forward. And I don't know about you, but that often leads me to have a one-way conversation with God. This monologue is usually one request after another. And as a result of this one-sided talk, nothing changes. I know God wants us to bring Him every thought and concern we have, but I know He is also longing for something else ... our praise and a thankful heart.

I was reminded of this when I read Psalms 113:3. "From the rising of the sun to its setting the name of the Lord is to be praised." The way I read it, that means all day. So I took on that challenge. For an entire day, all I did when I talked to the Lord was praise Him for who He is and what He has done in my life and the lives of those I love. Although there were many needs that presented themselves that day, I didn't take even one request to the Lord. Instead, when a need was brought to my mind, I focused and praised the Lord for that characteristic of Him that could solve the need. I was thanking Him for being the Great Physician, the Prince of Peace, the ultimate Counselor, the best problem solver, the One who prays for me, the Lover of my soul, the great I Am ... and the list went on and on. At the end of the day, I realized that I wasn't focusing on any of the problems that had come up that day. And then over the weekend, I watched God do the impossible and was again reminded that all things are truly possible through Him. Give it a try. Praise and thank God all day without requesting anything from Him. I can promise you that you'll be glad you did!

91...Face Time with God

Good morning! I had someone recently ask me why the title of my first devotional book was *Good Morning, Lord!* instead of good afternoon or good evening. My answer was really quite simple. I don't believe you should face the day until you have "Face Timed" with God.

I promise you that if you take a few minutes with God each morning, even before you get out of bed, you will be better equipped to handle whatever comes your way that day. Just acknowledging His presence will help you start your day with the correct mindset. Can you imagine how lame our excuses must sound to God when we don't take time for Him? It is like we're saying, "I don't have time to spend with you today. I'm just way too busy." But then just as soon as something happens in our day that makes us stumble, that's when we see the importance of spending time with God, and we want Him right there with us, helping us take care of the issue. God is not a genie in a bottle that we put in and take out based on our needs. He is *God* that is interested in having a relationship with *you.* And since conversation is important in a relationship, we should start our day out by talking to God.

Psalm 63:1 says,

> *O God, Thou art my God; I shall seek Thee earnestly; my soul thirsts for Thee, my flesh yearns for Thee, in a dry and weary land where there is no water.*

You always get more out of a relationship with God than you put in to it. Giving God a few minutes each morning will pay dividends all day long. So, here's to taking the time to invite God to go with you into your day!

92...Properly Clothed

Good morning! As I've already mentioned in earlier devotions, my favorite fishing vacation spot is Bennett Spring State Park. I was fortunate enough to get to go there twice in 2017. With any vacation, pictures help you remember the good times during the trip.

I was looking at my vacation pictures yesterday when I noticed something. I actually looked like a trout fisherman. I had all the essentials ... waders, vest, and a hat. My fishing vest had two pockets in the back and a clip that I hung my net on, and 15 assorted sized pockets on the front of the vest. I had all kinds of stuff in and hanging on those pockets. You need all of those different pockets to carry everything you might need instead of carrying a tackle box. But the most important thing I was wearing was the trout tag. That made me an official trout fisherman, so says the game warden ☺

It's important to be properly clothed in both fishing and in life. Colossians 3:12 tells us that as a Believer, we need to clothe ourselves with "compassion, kindness, humility, gentleness, and patience." And our clothing instructions continue in verse 14. "And beyond all these things put on love, which is the perfect bond of unity." If we successfully wear all of the above, others will be able to tell that we belong to God, and that's much better than being known as a fisherman, unless of course, you're fishing for lost souls. So, here's to being properly clothed to share our best with others!

93...PICKING YOUR DESTINATION

Good morning! While I was listening to the radio, the announcers began playing a game called, "Would you rather?" They would pose a question like, "Would you rather give up watching TV or reading books?" Sounded interesting, so I played along. I was like a seesaw on that first question. I love to read books but I also love to watch tennis on TV. Being on a seesaw on a silly game like this is OK because there's nothing at stake.

But let me ask you a "Would you rather" question that matters. "Would you rather spend eternity in paradise or in torment?" The story in Luke 16:19-31 tells about a man who chose to live in torment. Seeing Lazarus far away, the man cried out to Father Abraham asking if he could send Lazarus to him so that he could dip the tip of his finger in water and cool off his tongue. Then he continued by saying, "For I am in agony in this flame." As the story goes, the man was denied the request because it's impossible to cross over the chasm between Heaven and hell. The man then asked if Lazarus could go warn his five brothers who were still alive so that they wouldn't also come to this place of torment.

Hell is a real place and those that end up there, made a choice to do so. One of the reasons I write these morning texts is because I don't want anyone I know making that dreadful choice. There are so many reasons why choosing Jesus is the right choice, not only for the here and now, but for all eternity. If you haven't made that choice, there's no time like today to do so. Eternity is waiting for all of us, the destination is your choice. Here's to choosing Jesus … this is my prayer for you!

94...Arms Wide Open

Good morning! One thing that I'm sure we can all agree on is that life is unpredictable. Just when you think things are going smoothly, something will hit you right out of the blue and ***BAM!*** ... you experience the unpredictable. When that happens, who do you run to? I understand our need for a human touch when that happens but the better place to run *first* is always to the Lord.

When is the last time you felt wrapped up in the arms of God? Unfortunately, too many people believe that feeling of being held in His arms is something that only happens once or twice in a lifetime. Even many Christians have this wrong perception. Experiencing that isn't something that can only happen every once in a while. The Lord's arms are always wide open waiting to hold us close. The Lord wants to comfort us so that we can then show the same compassion and comfort we received from Him to others when they need it.

2 Corinthians 1:3-4 says,

> *Blessed be the God and Father of our Lord Jesus Christ, the Father of mercies and the God of all comfort; who comforts us in all our affliction so that we may be able to comfort those who are in any affliction with the comfort with which we ourselves are comforted by God.*

So, here's to following God's plan when the unexpected happens. Run to Him, receive His comfort, and be ready to share that compassion and comfort with others when they need it.

95...Free Flowing

Good morning! Have you ever been hurt by someone you thought you could trust? I'm sure we all have. That hurt might've cut right through you, it might've cost you a lot of money, or it just tried to take away your hope. When those situations happen, we may forget an important element in forgiving them.

Romans 5:5 says, "And hope does not disappoint, because the love of God has been poured out within our hearts through the Holy Spirit who was given to us." When we let God's love flow through us, it can spill out over all areas of our life. One of the best examples of unconditional love that we can show the world is when we forgive someone who has wronged us terribly. Since God has forgiven us of our transgressions, we are called to forgive others. Forgiving out of our own power doesn't happen. But because we have God's love in our hearts through the Holy Spirit, with Him we can then forgive others.

In both Gospels of Matthew and Mark there is a well-known story about Jesus taking five loaves of bread and two fishes and feeding a multitude of people with them. I like this analogy when it comes to love and forgiveness because they don't start to multiply until you give them away. It's a choice we all have to make when someone causes us pain. I can promise you that when you choose to forgive, God will be smiling down on you. So, here's to letting God's love flow freely through us!

96...God's Glory

Good morning! God's creations are absolutely amazing! One of the things I marveled at while I was on vacation was that all of the fishing waters at Bennett Spring State Park came from just one little spring. Really, just one little spring feeds it all! The ladies at the store there told me that over 100 million gallons of water comes from that spring each day. It starts with that one spring and then it branches off creating streams that give many different locations to fish in. I honestly don't know how people can say they don't believe in God when they look at things like this in nature.

In Psalm 19, David reflects on the glory of God. Verse 1 says, "The Heavens are telling of the glory of God; and their expanse is declaring the work of His hands." This verse reminds us that everywhere we look, we can see the glory of God. We just need to slow down enough and have our eyes open so we don't miss out on any of His glorious creations. The second stanza of the song, "How Great Thou Art" hits on this point:

> *When through the woods and forest glades I wander*
> *and hear the birds sing sweetly in the trees;*
> *When I look down from lofty mountain grandeurs*
> *and hear the brook and feel the gentle breeze;*
> *Then sings my soul, my Savior God to Thee:*
> *How great Thou art! How great thou art!*
> *Then sings my soul, my Savior God to Thee:*
> *How great Thou art! How great Thou art!*
> *Indeed, God is great!! Here's to singing of His glory.*

97...Healing Words

Good morning! Grief is a funny thing. Just when you think you have a handle on it, out of the blue it hits again. But just as it comes with no warning, so does the salve for that wound. Our spoken words can either add salt to the wound, or rush in like a breath of fresh air.

I'm very thankful that I have those in my life that cheer me on with their uplifting words. I wonder if they know that God sees them as wise?? Proverbs 12:18 says that reckless words pierce like a sword, "but the tongue of the wise brings healing." I want all of my words to be healing so I know I need to watch them carefully, especially when I'm struggling, for those are the times when I'm not as positive. Proverbs 12:25 says, "Anxiety in the heart of a man weighs it down, but a good word makes it glad."

Asking the Lord to guide my words before I talk is the best way I know how to insure my words will be beneficial to others. Not saying anything is so much better for me than saying the first thing that comes to mind. I guess that is what the verse in James 1:19 means when it says that we should be quick to listen, slow to speak and slow to become angry. So as we go through this day, my prayer for us is that we will ask the Lord to give us opportunities to be that breath of fresh air for someone who needs to be encouraged. And just as important, that the Lord will put His hand over our mouth when necessary so we can't spew out anything negative.

98...Perfect Plans

Good morning! "If there's a will, there's a way." We've all heard that saying before. I used to see this saying as a "me" directive. When problems would arise, I had to find a way to solve them within my own abilities. Sometimes, things would work out smoothly and other times, not so much. When I wasn't able to achieve what I set out to do, I would go to Plan B or C or ... you get the idea. There were even times that I ran through the entire alphabet and still was not able to achieve the desired result. I just couldn't get it done by myself.

Thankfully though, I now see this as a "God" directive. If it's His will, then He will provide the way. John 15:5 says, "I am the vine; you are the branches; He who abides in Me, and I in him, he bears much fruit; for apart from Me you can do nothing." When we let God handle things, we don't have to rely on our own abilities and limited resources.

With Jesus being the true Vine, we need to realize that as branches, we cannot do what God has called us to do without Him. And if God wants to involve us in the solution, He will give us the abilities and resources to get the job done. He will give us exactly what we need to produce the desired fruit. With God, we can rest assured that we don't need a Plan B because His plans are always perfect. So, here's to trusting and abiding in the Lord and going with the flow of His plan for our lives.

99...Raise a Fork

Good morning! Today I have the urge to bake a cake because it is Alan's birthday. It's another one of those bittersweet days. I'm thanking God for three things today.

The first one is for creating Alan and allowing him to live here for fifty-five years and that we know he's living in Heaven now. Secondly, I'm thanking God that He allowed Alan and I to be husband and wife. What a beautiful marriage He blessed us with! And finally, that Alan's life had such an impact on others. He lives on through the many lives he touched. But let's go back to number two for a moment. The reason Alan and I had such an amazing marriage is that we didn't look to each other to complete us. We understood that was God's role and we let Him have it. It was as though God was the cake and Alan was the icing on top.

I was reminded about this on Sunday when my pastor was talking about what it takes to be a dynamic disciple of Jesus. The first point he made was that we have no rivals in our love for Jesus. Even though I was aware of that, I see now that there were times when I had elevated Alan over Jesus. Times when I would run to Alan first and Jesus second. The reason I knew I did that is because with Alan now being gone, things have happened and the first thing I do is instinctively look for him. The Lord had been very sweet about showing me what I have done from time to time and He's helping me now to keep Him in His proper place. So, here's to following the second commandment found in Exodus 20:3. "You shall have no other gods before me." And if you have cake today, raise a fork and thank God for His beautiful creation, that we lovingly call, Alan.

100...Take Out the Trash

Good morning! Yesterday was my designated trash day and I was glad to get rid of it because it was stinking up my garage. When the garbage truck picked it up, I said "Good riddance!" Later that afternoon I thought about my response to my stinky trash being picked up when I read Matthew 11:28-30.

> *Come to Me, all who are weary and heavy-laden, and I will give you rest. Take My yoke upon you, and learn from Me, for I am gentle and humble in heart; and you shall find rest for your souls. For My yoke is easy, and My load is light.*

We like the first part of those verses but too often ignore the later portion. It's as though we want to put all our troubles in a garbage bag and dump them at the feet of Jesus and expect them to be hauled off. God doesn't work that way though. I can only imagine God thinks that "stinks" as He is wanting so much more.

He wants us, not just our garbage. He wants us to work with Him as He helps us through our trials. The problems we are facing may or may not go away but our thoughts and attitudes will change as we walk through our designated problems with Him. God is all about taking the situations of life and using them to draw us closer to Him. So, here's to dumping our trash on trash day but learning to rest in the Lord by loving, trusting, and standing on His promises as we go through the ups and downs of life.

101...Promises Kept

Good morning! Have you ever made a promise that you couldn't keep? I think we all have. We have the best intentions of doing exactly what we said we were going to do but then something happens that causes us not to be able to fulfill it.

I'm sure glad that we serve a God who keeps ALL of His promises. We have limitations that God doesn't have. When God makes a promise, He fulfills it ... 100% of the time. The Bible is full of promises that are made in the Old Testament and then we see them fulfilled in the New Testament. Let me give you one very well-known example. Isaiah 7:14 says, "Behold, a virgin will be with child and bear a son, and she will call His name Immanuel."

Then we see in the New Testament in Matthew 1:20-25 that the promise was fulfilled. Joseph was visited by an angel of the Lord in a dream. The angel told him not to be afraid to take Mary as his wife because what was conceived in her was from the Holy Spirit. So, Joseph arose and did what the angel commanded and took Mary to be his wife but kept her a virgin until their son was born, and then named him Jesus, thus fulfilling the promise found back in the book of Isaiah.

Knowing that God's promises are always kept, it's then so reassuring to know that if the Lord says He is going to prepare a place for us so we can be with Him forever, then we can look forward to living in Heaven with the Lord. Here's to being more like God and keeping our promises!

102...Standing Firm

Good morning! "Silence is golden." This old adage is as true today as it was when I was first told that as a little girl. I thought of that saying today when I was reading in the book of Exodus. Specifically, when I was reading the story about how God parted the Red Sea.

In Exodus 14, Moses was trying to convince the sons of Israel that they should not fear, even though the Egyptians were pursuing them and things weren't looking good at all. Exodus 14:14 was Moses' response to their complaining. "The Lord will fight for you while you keep silent." I'm sure that keeping silent wasn't what they had in mind.

Aren't we at times a lot like the sons of Israel? We trust God as long as what we can see looks promising. But as soon as we can't see what's happening, we start to get a little unnerved. We need to do what Moses was encouraging those people to do ... stand firm in your position until you see how God will handle the situation.

There is no need to drown ourselves in worry just because we don't know God's next move. And by the way, the sons of Israel could NEVER have imagined what God's next move was. Parting the Red Sea was totally a God thing. His solutions are far better than anything we could come up with. So, here's to giving God total control and watching with great anticipation for His next move!

103...A Forgiving Heart

Good morning! Forgiveness is one of those skills we need to practice almost daily. We need to extend it when we can't believe he just said that or when we're shocked that she just did that. Maybe they apologized or maybe they didn't. This could be an ongoing problem that causes us to forgive that person over and over again or this could be a *doozie*, one-time issue. Either way, we need to forgive.

Romans 5:8 gives us the reason why. "But God demonstrates His own love toward us, in that while we were yet sinners, Christ died for us." If Jesus would do that for us, we have no other choice but to forgive those who cause us pain. The best way to forgive is to do so immediately. But because of our flawed ways, we too often have to chew on the hurt awhile before we're ready to spit it out. Doing that causes us needless pain and actually adds to the original hurt.

Sometimes, the hurt is so deep that all we can do is tell the Lord we want to forgive the offender but don't know how. That puts our hearts in the right spot for God to do what He does best ... love us to that point of forgiveness. After all, while we were still hurting the Lord through our sinful ways, He offered to forgive us. When we look at our hurt from that point of view, our only choice is to forgive others. So, as we start this day, using Jesus as our example, my prayer is that we make the choice to extend a forgiving heart to anyone that hurts us along the way.

104...Sleep Well

Good morning! When we look up a word in the dictionary, we not only get the definition but also an example of the word, too. The definition of the word **unknown** is "not known or familiar." The best example of that word for me is ... life.

From day to day, we don't know what will happen in our lives and it's often that unknown that can keep us awake at night. But we don't need to lose sleep over those things just because we don't know how they will turn out. Joshua 1:9 says, "Have I not commanded you? Be strong and courageous! Do not tremble or be dismayed, for the Lord your God is with you wherever you go."

No matter what the storm in our life is, we don't have to weather it alone. Whether you're searching for medical answers, wondering if you will be able to financially keep your house, or how much longer your current situation will last, we don't have to handle these isolated showers alone because we know the One who controls them all.

Our Heavenly Father has all the resources on the earth to do with as He pleases. And no matter how long our current situation has been going on, this life is just like a flash of lightning compared to the storm-free life that we are promised as Believers for all eternity. So, instead of running one scenario after another through our minds at night, here's to thanking the Lord for all He is and for all He does on our behalf and then drifting off to a restful night of sleep!

105...Setting Fear Aside

Good morning! We always seem to like it when someone says, "I've got good news for you!" Life can bring us some of the most exciting news, like the birth of a child, or a promotion at work, or getting married. On the flip side of that coin, life also can bring devastating news. Sometimes in life it seems like the old phrase, "when it rains, it pours," is all too accurate. Where good news seems like nothing but blue skies, bad news often seems like it's just a long, dark, lonely tunnel. It is as though there is no end in sight.

But as Christians, we need to remember that even if the tunnel of bad news is long, it's definitely not lonely or dark. Because where there is God, there is hope, and Romans 5:1–5 tells us that hope does not disappoint. Since the Lord is always with us, we can't go through anything alone, which means we are not alone in the tunnel. And just as reassuring, there's not only light at the end of the tunnel, but all the way through the tunnel, too. Oh, how I praise God for these truths!

Psalm 112:7 tells us why we don't have to fear bad news. "He will not fear evil tidings [bad news]; his heart is steadfast, trusting in the Lord." When we put our trust in the Lord, we no longer have to be afraid of the news lurking right around the corner. Jesus is our rock and He will walk every step of life's journey with us, even when that journey takes us through a long tunnel. So, here's to setting fear aside and trusting the Lord!

106...No Phone Necessary

Good morning! This week, I discovered just how much I depend on my cell phone when it stopped working. I use my phone as my clock, my alarm, my calendar and the place where I keep my notes. It's my lifeline to the outside world. All of my contacts are listed there so I can communicate with others via phone calls, texts, or emails. I also have many pictures in my phone and that's why it made me sick when I thought I lost my pictures of Alan.

I also use my phone as part of my ministry. I type out my morning devotions and send them from my phone. Thankfully, everything was backed up from my phone to the "cloud" so I didn't lose anything and now it's safe to continue to be dependent on it. ☺ Being dependent on my phone is trivial compared to being dependent on God. His word teaches us that He wants us to be totally dependent on Him. The Lord wants us to bring every thought, need, desire and question to Him. God is always there for us.

He wants to fight our battles, if we let Him. Isaiah 26:4 says, "Trust in the Lord forever, for in God the Lord, we have an everlasting Rock." Psalm 121:2 clearly states where we should turn. "My help comes from the Lord, who made Heaven and earth." So, if the God that created Heaven and earth, and all that is in it, wants us to be dependent on Him, then my prayer is that we would be wise enough to do just that. The Lord is my rock and fortress in whom I take refuge because He's shown me time and time again that it's safe to depend on Him. So, here's to being able to call upon the Lord anytime … no phone required!

107...Eclipse 2017

Good morning! It's finally here ... Eclipse 2017. We've been hearing about this historical day for many months now, and today, a total solar eclipse will be happening right over where I live in Southeast Missouri. People from other parts of the country are coming into our area to see the moon block the sun.

In Scripture, you will find lots of metaphors showing how our sin blocks the Son's Light in our life. In these comparisons, sin is referred to as the darkness and in contrast, 1 John 1:5 tells us about the Light. "And this is the message we have heard from Him and announce to you, that God is light, and in Him there is no darkness at all." Since Light and darkness can't co-exist, how do we handle this dilemma in our life? Since we all are sinners, sin will be in our life, no matter how much we wish it wouldn't be. But as Believers, we are redeemed sinners. Jesus paid the price of our sins on the cross and therefore, when we confess our sins, God is quick to forgive us and thus lets His Light shine through us again.

There are several ways to view today's eclipse safely. Many will wear the special glasses and some will use the box with the tiny pin hole so just a little light can come through. That little pin box reminds me of a life of unconfessed sin. God is still our Light but our sins only allow a tiny, tiny bit of His Light to enter our lives. The total solar eclipse will last for a short time but God doesn't want us to walk in darkness for any length of time. So here's to doing our part to live in the Light of our Heavenly Father by being quick to confess our sins and then turn away from the darkness. May His Light shine bright in you.

108...Being Aware

Good morning! I was thinking this morning about the shark we had in our aquarium. I was always amazed at how he could live with the other fish without any problems. Sure, he would chase the other fish from time to time but most of the time he was calm. Alan had put a coffee mug on its side and covered it with rock so it would have a place to go and chill out. Over the years, we'd find a floating fish occasionally but didn't think too much of it. Recently though, the shark was getting so big and fish were disappearing. I'll let you connect those dots. When I cleaned out the aquarium, I found out where parts of those fish had been. You guessed it ... in the coffee mug. Yep, there was a reason for the shark's increase in size.

In our Christian life, we also need to be aware of our enemy. Satan moves in and out of our lives, often subtly. He might chase us around a bit or try to just blend into the normal routines of our day, waiting for an opening to pounce. Make no mistake, he is a shark and has come for one reason and one reason only. Satan is here to kill, steal, and destroy. He wants to keep as many people as he can from spending eternity with the Lord. The good news though is that God has other plans for us. John 10:10 says, "The thief comes only to steal, and kill, and destroy; I came that they might have life, and might have it abundantly." Just as we need to be aware that the enemy is lurking around waiting for the perfect opportunity to attack, we need to also remember that God has won this war over the enemy and has offered us abundant life in Him. So, here's to praying that in your life the score is God-WON, shark-ZERO!

109...In Jesus' Name

Good morning! Day to day little things happen that can be irritating. Yesterday, my phone quit and so did my aquarium. Even though it took up the majority of my day, I was able to deal with both situations. Just like with all problems, God always has something to show us. With my phone going out, it made me consider getting a land line for emergencies. I've been thinking about getting rid of the aquarium before this happened. It was good for a season but now that season is over. I'm thinking that both the phone and aquarium were hit by a power surge. But when I thanked the Lord that nothing else was affected, a thought came to mind.

We pray for things in the name of Jesus as John 14:13 instructs us. I learn by examples and remember things the same way. So as I ended my prayer I used examples of what Jesus has done through stories in the Bible and my life. My prayer went something like this. "Lord, thank you so much for using these minor inconveniences to show me things I needed to take care of. I'm thankful that nothing else was hurt with the power surge. I ask that You continue to keep me safe in my home. And I pray all of this ... (this is where I usually would end the prayer by saying "in your precious name" but instead I closed by saying the following) ... in the name of the One who healed the man blind from birth, who also healed the woman who bled for years, and the same One who is healing me. Amen." It's important to remind ourselves of all the reasons we do pray in Jesus' name and for me this is how I want to end my prayers from now on. It'll keep all He has done for me right in the front of my mind. Maybe it'll work for you, too!

110...THE UPPER HAND

Good morning! There is always entertainment at my place from watching the animals around here. My ring doorbell, which alerts me that something is moving in front of my house, went off. When I looked outside to see who it was, to my surprise it was my dog, Cope, at the end of the sidewalk barking at one of my neighbor's bulls across the lane. It was a hilarious picture because the bull was not happy with Cope and Cope was irritated at the bull for whatever reason, but confident he could successfully take on the bull.

Do you ever take on something that's too big for you? This reminded me of the story of David and Goliath found in 1 Samuel Chapter 17. Standing back and looking at those two, it appeared that David would not stand a chance against the enormous Goliath. But David had one thing that Goliath didn't have ... the favor of God. As the Bible story goes, David killed Goliath with one stone and a sling shot. This story serves as a reminder that when God is with us, we have everything we could possibly need.

As far as the situation with my dog and the bull, Cope was about to bite off more than he could chew, since he only weighs about 25 pounds and the bull weighs closer to 1,000 pounds. It took some convincing on my part, be he finally gave up the fight and I was able to keep him safe. No matter what your physical stature is, here's to always having the upper hand in the battles of life by making sure we have God with us!

111...Lose the Luggage

Good morning! As I was waiting to meet a friend for lunch, I overheard a conversation at the next table. They were talking about luggage issues they had with their recent flight. It's kind of hard to travel without luggage. Some airlines charge you for the bags you take and most put a weight limit on each bag. When my California family would visit, they always had more stuff going home than their luggage could hold. Alan had been given some Marlboro travel bags and they became the overflow luggage. Those Marlboro bags were easy to spot on the luggage carousel and they had more frequent flyer miles than I ever had.

We also travel with baggage every single day and the weight of our baggage seems to have no limits. Sometimes, we don't even recognize the baggage we are carrying with us. That baggage comes from negative experiences that have happened in our past. Alan and I always called that baggage our "giants." But the difference between us and the luggage we take when we travel is that we don't have to travel with the daily baggage.

Jesus has given us a way to lose that baggage and live without the weight of it through His ultimate sacrifice on the cross. In Luke 9:62, Jesus is telling us that we should not look back to our past sins and failures, but rather to keep our eyes focused ahead in faith through Jesus. "But Jesus said to him, 'No one, after putting his hand to the plow and looking back, is fit for the kingdom of God.'" Jesus wants to get rid of our baggage, as we keep our hands on the plow, looking forward and letting go of the past. So, here's to letting the Lord take care of our giants!

Good morning! By listening to people, you can often tell where they are from. Either their accent or what they call things can help you determine where they live. East coast people refer to soda as "pop" and the amount of drawl on your words will help others see how far south you live. But there are differences within any given area, too. Alan and his dad used to give me trouble over what I called meal times. I grew up calling our meals breakfast, lunch and dinner. Alan grew up calling them breakfast, dinner and supper. You can see where the confusion came in over when "dinner" occurred. They had lots of fun with that.

I'm glad that God is crystal clear when He tells us what it takes to spend eternity in Heaven with Him. It doesn't matter what part of the country, or world for that matter, that you live in. The exact same thing is required by all to become a child of God. Romans 3:23 tells us that we all have sinned and fallen short of the glory of God. And as a result Romans 6:23 tells us that "the wages of sin is death but the free gift of God is eternal life in Christ Jesus our Lord." So what can we do about our sin debt? Romans 10:9 says "that if you confess with your mouth Jesus as Lord, and believe in your heart that God raised Him from the dead, you will be saved." And Romans 10:13 sums it up by saying for "WHOEVER WILL CALL UPON THE NAME OF THE LORD WILL BE SAVED." I love how God makes it so clear for us. In my Bible, He put the last verse in all caps so we couldn't miss it. Thanking God today for His clarity and the opportunity He gives us to be forever with Him!

113...Food for Thought

Good morning! As I was going to town today, there were two homeless people at the highway exit holding signs that said they were homeless and hungry. I have to be honest, I've driven past others holding signs asking for help many times. But today, the man holding the sign was also motioning with his hands that he just wanted something to eat. As I drove by, I saw him say, "Please!" When I asked God what I should do, before He could answer, I immediately started coming up with excuses not to give the man money. I've heard that some of these people make a really good living camping out at exits. Others, I've been told, use the money to buy drugs or alcohol.

After the excuses ran out, I heard the Lord remind me of the verses in Matthew 25:35-40 where on judgement day the Lord separates the sheep from the goats. To the sheep on His right He says, "Come, you who are blessed of My Father, inherit the kingdom prepared for you from the foundation of the world. For I was hungry, and you gave me something to eat ..." And when they asked the Lord when they ever fed Him, His response was, "Truly I say to you, to the extent that you did it to one of these brothers of Mine, even the least of them, you did it to Me." As I made a loop around the exit, tears started flowing. When I got back to where the man was again, I pulled out all the money I had on me, $8. It wasn't much but I'll never forget his face when I handed him the money. You would have thought I gave him a hundred thousand dollars. All I know is that I received a much greater blessing than that homeless man did today. It's just food for thought ...

114...Keeping Focused

Good morning! Today being Wednesday is what is commonly known as "hump day." It's the middle of the work week for many, so half of the week is over. Only a few more days of work and then you can do what you want. When I was teaching, and it was getting close to the end of the school year, I would make a calendar on my board and we would mark off each day to the end of the school year. And then we'd be free for the summer. Looking back at that now, boy was my thought process skewed, and yours might be, too.

Ask yourself this question, "What's my purpose at my workplace?" Or for that matter, what's our purpose in life? Matthew 17:18 says, "As Thou didst send Me into the world, I also have sent them into the world." (We are the "them.") This verse confirms that Jesus was purposely sent into the world with a specific mission, or job, to do. We see through the pages of the Bible that Jesus was always mindful of His mission.

Using His life as an example, we have also been purposely sent to do the Father's work, which is carrying His message of hope to a world that desperately needs Jesus. God has given us a mission field within our workplace. Jesus never took a weekend or a summer off. He was always about the Father's business. No matter what you do each day, whether it be a Monday or a Friday, a workday or a vacation day, our life's purpose needs to be the focus of what we do. So, here's to asking the Lord to help us keep the purpose He has called us to in the front of our mind, and letting everything else take a backseat!

115...God's Own Words

Good morning! We've all heard the phrase, "What doesn't kill you, makes you stronger." As raw as that sounds, it is true. Too often though we want to play the "blame game" when life is hard and obstacles are many. We want to shift any responsibility we might have played into being totally someone else's fault. We even blame God for allowing those circumstances to happen in our lives or for not stopping them once they started. We want to know why something is happening because we think if we know the "why" then it would be easier to handle.

The prevailing thought back in Biblical times was that when something bad was going on, it was because of the sin in that person's life. I love the story of the blind man found in John 9:1-12. The disciples asked Jesus whose sin caused this man to be blind, his parents or his. In verse 3 Jesus responded by saying, "It was neither that this man sinned, nor his parents; but it was in order that the works of God might be displayed in him."

Jesus kicked that old thought pattern right out the window. Being reminded of that answer by Jesus sure does help in challenging times. I know that we need the help of the Holy Spirit daily to check our lives for any sin that might be there and take corrective actions to right those wrongs, but it's comforting to think that the difficulties in our life might just be so God's work can be displayed through us. So, when hard times come, here's to using God's own words to bring us peace!

116...Bringing Us Home

Good morning! One of the things Alan and I enjoyed doing was taking a drive in the country. He'd try to get me lost on the county roads and in the beginning, he was very successful, but I got better at finding the way back home as the years went on. I was reminded of this as I took a friend to church with me. She lives out on those same county roads. When I picked her up, it was daylight. When I took her home, it was dark. Did you know that you can't follow bread crumbs in the dark??? LOL ☺

Needless to say, I got quite lost on those county roads. Around every corner, I thought I'd see something that was familiar, so I kept driving. Twenty minutes later, I finally ended up on familiar road. From there, I was good to go. Fifteen minutes more and I was home safe and sound. Alan would have been laughing. ☺

Spiritually speaking, have you ever felt lost? You know, when you just feel like you are going through the motions, but nothing truly is happening. One thing I love about our Heavenly Father is that no matter how many times we veer off the path He has laid out for us, He always brings us back, if we let Him. We don't have to stumble in the dark, when we can live in the Light. Ephesians 5:8 says, "For you were formally darkness, but now you are light in the Lord; walk as children of light." So, when we feel lost, we need to go with what we know, the familiar Light of Jesus, and He will lead us safely home!

117...Son-Shine

Good morning! Do you remember those times when you were little and you just didn't want to go to bed because you thought you would miss out on something? Sometimes it was still light outside, which didn't help matters much. I was reminded of those times when a group from my church talked about their mission trip to Alaska.

As they were sharing how God moved and stirred hearts during their trip, they talked about things they had to get accustomed to while they were there. One thing that stayed with me was that there was 24 hours of sunlight. I wouldn't ever want to sleep having that much daylight. Think of all the things you could get done in the course of a day with all that sunshine, assuming you could physically get by with not sleeping. I wouldn't know how to act with that much light.

But one day I will experience Light forever. Isaiah 60:19 says,

No longer will you have the sun for light by day, not for brightness will the moon give you light; but you will have the Lord for an everlasting light, and your God for your glory.

One day, all Christians will live in constant light because the Lord will be the One shining in Heaven. Until that day comes, having the 24 hours of sunshine a day in Alaska is the closest we'll get to what we will experience in Heaven with constant light. I wonder if the Believers who live in Alaska have thought of that? Anyway, until that day comes for each of us, here's to letting the Son-shine!

118...Faith Walk

Good morning! I'm sure we all can agree that from time to time in life we just don't understand why things are happening. As I'm watching friends who are going through some really tough times right now, I'm reminded that some of the greatest lessons that I have learned in my life and that have strengthened my faith have come during those rough patches.

Jesus is an amazing teacher, but we don't get to pick the classes we are put in. None of us would pick classes like cancer, the loss of a child, or divorce, but sometimes that is where we find ourselves. What I have found in my life is those tougher classes are the ones that have made me stronger and have given me the knowledge on how to handle future tough times.

Even though those times were rough, I wouldn't trade them for anything now as they helped me trust the Lord more. In 2 Corinthians 5:7, the Lord tells us that we need to walk by faith and not by sight. It's easy to walk by faith when everything is hunky-dory in your life, but when unwelcome troubles arise, that's when we need our faith walk. The prerequisite for handling those unwanted classes is to recall how God has carried you through previous tough times. So, here's to being 110% sure that our God is both faithful and trustworthy!

119...Rocking with Confidence

Good morning! I was recently at a Crackle Barrel Restaurant and it was packed, so I had to wait outside. As I waited to go inside, I was standing by a lot of people on the front porch. They were discussing life and their concerns, while rocking in the many available rocking chairs. Listening to them reminded me of something I've always heard growing up. Worry is like a rocking chair. It gives you something to do, but it gets you nowhere.

Scripture tells us the exact same thing, just worded differently. Proverbs 12:25 tells us" Anxiety in the heart of a man weighs it down, but a good word makes it glad." Based on the conversations I overheard, it seemed the uncertainties of life was what was causing the anxiety and worry. Concern over what the doctor's report was going to say, and whether or not their retirement money will run out too soon, and some political issues were also being discussed. In general, they were trying to solve the problems of this world, all of which were totally out of their control.

With God as our Heavenly Father, we can live in confidence that He has everything under His control. While we might not understand it all, we can trust in His promises and provisions. If we truly trust the Lord to be in charge of everything in our lives, then we can bypass all of that worrying and fretting. So, next time you find yourself in a rocking chair, let your words of confidence bring gladness to the hearts of those listening.

120...Clearing Hurdles

Good morning! There is a family of deer living in the woods behind my house. Every once in a while, when I'm driving down my lane, I'll have to stop for the deer as they cross the road. They jump over one fence, hit the road once or twice, and then gracefully glide over the second fence as they go back to the woods.

They remind me of my days of running track in school. There is a big difference though. When I would run hurdles, from time to time I would catch my back foot on the hurdle as I tried to clear it and would knock it over. That wasn't the case with those deer. They didn't miss a beat as they successfully cleared the fence each time.

I like the verse in Psalms which tells us that when we stumble in our walk with the Lord that He will keep us from falling because He holds our hand. But we must preface that with the condition found in the previous verse. Psalm 37:23 says, "The steps of a man are established by the Lord; and He delights in his way." In other words, in order not to fall completely on our face when we mess up, we must delight ourselves in the Lord.

I don't know if you have any faith hurdles to clear, but I do know that we have the Lord that is willing to help us glide right over them. All we have to do is swallow our pride and ask for His help. He is always there waiting to give us the assistance we need, if we just ask. So, here's to a day without stumbles!

121...Carrying One Another's Burdens

Good morning! Today being September 11, we find our country mourning loss once again from forces out of our control. This time the force is a hurricane named Irma. There are millions of Americans being affected by this natural disaster. But as terrible as this storm is, my heart was warmed yesterday afternoon. I was driving north on I-55 and the traffic was light. Then all of a sudden that changed. Around a bend on I-55 going south, a huge caravan appeared. There must have been twenty utility trucks, half a dozen flat beds carrying large equipment, four or five semi-trucks carrying supplies, and what looked like medical vans. In this country, we argue and fight over the craziest things but when push comes to shove, people are willing to help one another in times of great peril. Just like after 9-11 happened, first responders are in place and are going in to help the victims.

Galatians 6:2 tells us to "bear one another's burdens, and thus fulfill the law of Christ." Those who are a part of the recovery effort are indeed bearing the burdens of others. Not everyone has been called to do what they are doing but something EVERYONE can do to have a positive impact on what's happening is to pray. Pray for the victims, the first responders, the recovery teams, the government, and anyone involved with this crisis. We have a God who is bigger than any Hurricane Harvey or Hurricane Irma. So, as we watch the devastation unfold on TV, let's do what we can do to help by praying.

122...Starting Young

Good morning! We've had a lot of thunderstorms lately. As I was lying in bed listening to the thunder rolling in, I remembered as a child being told that the thunder just meant people were bowling in Heaven. As a child, I accepted that explanation. And when the lightning would strike, I was told, you can probably guess it, someone just bowled a strike. When you stop and think about it, we were told a lot of crazy things when we were little, and as adults, we still remember them.

We need to make sure that we tell kids accurate things about Jesus from a very, very young age. When they get older and reflect back on their childhood, my prayer is that they'll never be able to remember a time when they didn't know about Jesus. Parents are either going to raise their children up to follow the world or to follow Jesus.

Deuteronomy 6:5-9 and 11:19 tell us that we need to take the Word of God and put it in our hearts and to make sure that we pass that Word on to our children and grandchildren. I'm so proud of my son and daughter in-law. They are teaching their girls about Jesus. When Alan died, they used that time to explain to their then almost two-year-old that her grandpa was with Jesus in Heaven. Now she's almost three and she tells me that often. Children are never too young to start hearing about Jesus. So, here's to using every opportunity we're given to pass the Word of God on to our children and grandchildren because when they're an adult, they'll remember what you've told them!

123...TEAMWORK

Good morning! I'm in the process of getting my garage finished out. One of my brothers and my sister in-law spent a day with me cleaning out the stuff in the garage. Then my oldest brother took over the next day. There is insulation to put up, followed by the drywall, then primed and painted. The finished garage will look great but it's a process that will take some time and teamwork.

When I was thanking God for the teamwork that's happening, it struck me that I experience teamwork every day in the Trinity of God the Father, God the Son, and God the Holy Spirit. Matthew 28:19 says, "Go therefore and make disciples of all the nations, baptizing them in the name of the Father and the Son and the Holy Spirit." Have you ever thought about the teamwork that was necessary for us to have the chance to be in right standing with God?

All parts of the Trinity have their own roles to play to achieve their desired result of giving us the opportunity to have the hope of salvation through the shed blood of Jesus. God the Father created the plan, Jesus implemented the plan, and the Holy Spirit administered the plan. My prayer for us as we go through this day is that we find time to thank the Father, Son, and Holy Spirit for the sacrifice and teamwork they so freely give us!

124...A Joyful Heart

Good morning! Do you ever crack yourself up when nobody else is around? I sure do! The other night I was thinking about what to have for dinner and I decided on roast, potatoes, and **dirt**. I have a couple of girlfriends that think pickled beets smell and taste like dirt, so I'll laugh about that every time I eat them. After dinner I was watching tennis. Alan and my son used to always tease me about how I would verbally "help" the players and officials. They would say the neighbors were calling to see if something was wrong because they heard a lot of commotion coming from our direction. Oh, by the way, we live at the end of a private lane. LOL ☺

As I was helping Venus Williams win her match, my dog on the front porch started whining. I looked over and he was staring at me through the window. I had to laugh when I said, "Not you too, Cope!" So, I opened the window and explained to him what happens when tennis is on. This is his first tennis season being on the front porch. ☺

I have found throughout my life that laughter is good for the soul. Proverbs 17:22 says, "A joyful heart is good medicine." I know laughter doesn't change circumstances but it does lighten them for a bit. In my mind, it isn't a good day without lots of laughter. That's one thing I really miss about Alan because we sure did laugh a lot.

As you go through this day, I hope you find plenty of reasons to have a good belly laugh or two!

125...Today Only

Good morning! I really enjoy watching the HGTV channel. One of the shows I like to watch focuses on beach front living. I didn't realize how many beach front areas there are in our country and I really like seeing all the different locations. On one of the shows, the family looking for the property was shown on the beach playing with their kids and their dog. It was the dog that got my attention. He had completely buried his head in the sand!

How many times have you wished you could do the same thing instead of dealing with life? We have all kinds of things to deal with on a daily basis. And if we would only focus on what was happening today, I think we'd be fine. When we start trying to deal with what we *think* is coming tomorrow, next week, next month, etc. is when we get overloaded and want to stick our head in the sand, just like the dog did. Matthew 6:34 tells us, "Therefore do not be anxious for tomorrow; for tomorrow will care for itself. Each day has enough trouble of its own." So true, so true.

Living a simple life requires us to release our perceived issues for future days into God's very capable hands. God just wants us to take life 24 hours at a time and focus on walking through each day with Him. Our minds can get really bogged down when we let them start wandering. Many of the catastrophes we think will happen, never do, so it's wasted energy to be concerned about them today. Let us ask God to show us what's on today's plan and leaving the rest alone!

126...Our Food Source

Good morning! From time to time at my place, there are animals that upset the peaceful existence that is usually found at my home. Last year the squirrels tore up everything I planted on my deck and were always eating the bird seed in the bird feeders. This year I did not plant anything on my deck and I moved the bird feeders to the front of my house. Thinking that I had the problem solved, I hung three bird feeders on two shepherd hooks.

Well, you guessed it, the squirrels are trying to eat out of those feeders. Since I don't want to hurt the squirrels and I just want to guide them away to a different food source, I came up with Plan B. I got this idea from a video my sister had sent me. I zip-tied a Slinky (Remember that toy?) to the top of the shepherd hook. The Slinky hangs about halfway down the hook, long enough that a squirrel can reached the bottom of it. When the squirrel starts climbing up the shepherd hooks and grabs a hold of the Slinky, it drops to the ground and the squirrel can't get up to the feeders. The more the squirrel tries to master climbing up the Slinky, the more he ends up on the ground.

I have to admit, getting the squirrel's attention this way was quite comical to watch. I'm sure at times the Lord thinks we're quite comical, too, as He tries to get our attention. The Holy Spirit doesn't want to hurt us either, just gently guide us to the Source that feeds us well. Jesus says in John 6:35, "I am the bread of life; he who comes to Me shall not hunger, and he who believes in Me shall never thirst." So, here's to knowing our best food source ... Jesus!

127...Giving Thanks

Good morning! Today we start one of my favorite months of the year ... November. Growing up, this was the beginning of the holiday season at my house. My mom's birthday started things off. Then one week later was my brother's and my birthday (yes, I was born on his first birthday! I was the best birthday present that he received! LOL). And the following week was Thanksgiving. It was a month full of family and celebration.

Even though my parents, Alan, and others that made this month special are gone, I still love the month of November. My oldest granddaughter now celebrates her birthday on the same day as mine, which is really cool, but that's not the reason why I still love this month. I now see November as the month of thanksgiving. Scripture tells us in 1 Thessalonians 5:18 that "in everything give thanks; for this is God's will for you in Christ Jesus." It's easy to give thanks for the good things in life. We can do that without giving it much thought at all. But when it comes to giving thanks for the hard things, that's a different story. It's hard to thank God for loved ones that have passed on, even when we understand that being in Heaven is the best place for them. It's challenging to give thanks for that family member that's just a thorn in your side, even though we know that the thorn is there because they need Jesus. And it's equally as difficult to thank God when those you love are hurting and there's nothing you can do about it. But just because it's hard doesn't mean we get a pass on being thankful. Like everything else in our faith, being thankful is a choice. My prayer for us is that through this month of November, we will intentionally give thanks each and every day to the Lord for everything in our life...the easy and the hard.

128...His Footprints

Good morning! Every day I look forward to going outside to check out the new grass that is growing in my backyard. I'm thrilled at how good it looks and then chuckle over how thick the grass is. When I bought the grass seed, I wasn't sure about how much seed I'd need because I wasn't able to tell the salesman the size of my backyard. I'm not good with sizes or distances so the salesman said to just start with ten pounds. So he weighed out ten pounds and I was eager to get home and get the seed spread around the backyard. A couple of days after the ten pounds of seed had been sown, I found out that I only needed about two pounds of seed for the size of my backyard. It's no wonder then why the grass is coming up super thick! ☺

Isaiah 43:19 says, "Behold, I will do something new, now it will spring forth; will you not be aware of it? I will even make a roadway in the wilderness, rivers in the desert." God is always working life's details out for us. Everyday there is something new He is doing on our behalf.

The question we need to ponder is, "Do we see Him moving in our lives?" It might not always be as easy to see as thick grass, but when we go through our days looking with great anticipation for what God is doing, we will start seeing His footprints in our lives. So, here's to thanking God for the roadways He's creating for us and asking Him to give us the eyes to see His amazing work in our day-to-day lives!

129...Leave it to God

Good morning! As I was praying for some dear friends who are going through a hard season of life, a song came on the radio by Natalie Grant that made me just stop on a dime. I realized I was doing it again...giving God possible solutions or answers to the prayer I'd prayed. Natalie Grant's song, "King of the World," has a chorus that sure got my attention.

When did I forget that You've always been the King of the world?
I tried to take life back right out of the hands of the King of the world.
How can I make You so small when You're the one who holds it all?
When did I forget that You've always been the King of the world?

Psalm 47:7 says, "For God is the King of all the earth; sing praises with a skillful psalm." The first part of this verse confirms that God is the King of the world, but it was the second part of that verse that was helpful to me with how I should pray. After I present a prayer request to the Lord, instead of trying to help Him with the answer to that prayer, or in other words, as the song says, trying to make Him so small by my limited possible answers, that I should sing praises to Him. It doesn't matter how well you sing because it all sounds great to God. I was also reminded of something my mom used to tell me when I was little. She said that singing was praying twice, and she was absolutely right. I need to remember these things when I pray. So, here's to making our prayer requests known to God and then just leaving the rest to Him as we sing praises to our Lord!

130...Focus on the Lord

Good morning! In life, seasons come and seasons go. Now that the calendar says we are officially in spring, we are starting to see changes. I love watching new life popping up everywhere. I also love the fact that as seasons change, the birds' coloring also changes. I have three bird feeders that I can see from my kitchen window and lately I've had a lot to look at. The yellow finches are turning a brighter yellow daily and the cardinals and chickadees are increasing in numbers.

Seeing changes in nature is just one area of change during seasons. During our lifetime, we will also experience personal seasons. Some of those seasons could be like periods of grief, nine months of pregnancy, a period of sickness, or retirement. During happy seasons, it's easy to rejoice and be joyful. But during those tougher seasons, do people see us reflect God's love to others or are we like a bear being forced to come out of hibernation?

1 Thessalonians 5:16 tells us to "rejoice always." There's no caveat where the "always" is concerned. This is definitely one of those crystal clear instructions. If you're in a tough season, even though you don't like what's going on, you can still remain joyful. And the only way I know to remain joyful during those times is by keeping my focus on the Lord and not the season itself. The flip side of that coin, where my focus is more on the season and less on the Lord, has never worked out well for me. So as a new season begins, here's to keeping our focus and walking it with the Lord!

131...Free Will

Good morning! I was recently reminded of the old adage, "You can lead a horse to water, but you can't make him drink." This literally happened with my horse. Alan always took care of our horses. And with him gone, I had to make the hard decision to find new homes for them. As my last horse was being picked up by his new owner, I tried to get her to drink some water before she was loaded in the horse trailer. She refused. I tried several ways to trick her into getting a drink but none worked. She knew something was going on and she wanted no part of it. Such is life. It's called having free will.

God also gives us free will. He gives us His word to live by and the Holy Spirit to help us live out His word, but what He doesn't do is force us or manipulate us in doing what He knows to be best for us. In other words, He doesn't try to force us to make the right decision, like I tried to do with my horse. We get to make that choice ourselves. Psalm 119:108 says, "O accept the free will offerings of my mouth, O Lord, and teach me Thine ordinances." The psalmist was praising God and vowing to follow His word.

The cool thing about having free will is that we get to love God with all our heart, not because we're told to, but because we want to. Isn't it nice to hear from those people we love that they also love us? God is no different. It warms His heart to hear His children tell Him they love Him. So, as we go through this day, let's use our free will and let God and others know they are loved!

132...STANDING STRONG

Good morning! There are times in our lives when we're not strong. The lack of strength could be physical, emotional, or spiritual. When those periods of time cross our path, it's good to have others who will stand in the gap for us.

I was reading the story of Moses when he was experiencing one of those times of weakness. The story is found in Exodus 17:8-16. There was a battle between the Amalek and Israel. Verses 11-12 say, "So it came about when Moses held his hand up, that Israel prevailed, and when he let his hand down, Amalek prevailed. But Moses' hands were heavy. Then they took a stone and put it under him, and he sat on it; and Aaron and Hur supported his hands, one on one side and one on the other. Thus, his hands were steady until the sun set."

So on top of the hill, when Moses would hold the staff of God up in his hand, they were victorious in their battle. But Moses became physically tired and wasn't able to continue keeping his hands lifted up. Now here's my favorite part of this story. Moses had a couple of friends with him to hold him up quite literally when he was too fatigued to continue by himself. They stood in the gap for Moses and held his arms up when he physically couldn't. How cool is that? I pray that you have those type of people in your life … family and/or friends that will hold you up when you are weak. If not, be that strength for someone else and watch what happens. God will bless you for it. Here's to being willing to be used by God to help others stand strong!

133...SITTING ON GO

Good morning! What sounds better to you, $9.99 or $10? What about 365 days or one year? It's all about your perspective, isn't it? Have you ever wondered why some people refuse to accept the Lord's invitation for salvation, especially with how crazy this world is becoming? For those of us who have accepted the gift of salvation and know that Heaven is our forever home, it's often hard for us to understand why anyone would want anything but that.

Before we accepted the path that Jesus made possible for us, we most likely had the same false perceptions as those who haven't accepted Jesus yet. Do you remember some of your perceptions at that time? You might have thought things like you could never see yourself as being good enough or you thought that God would never forgive your wheel barrel full of sins. And maybe you thought if you became a Christian, the days of you having any fun would be over. But then, someone came along side you and started speaking truths in your life and you started wondering if maybe your perceptions had been wrong.

As Believers, we are the living example of Christ. Those who have yet to come to faith watch us carefully to see if our words match up with our actions. 1 Peter 3:15 says, "but sanctify Christ as Lord in your hearts, always being ready to make a defense to everyone who asks you to give an account for the hope that is in you ..." We are here on this earth to further God's Kingdom. Just like someone helped us see God's perception on life and death, we are called to be ready to help others see life from God's point of view. Are you prepared to do that? I pray we will always be ready and sitting on "Go"!

134...Victorious

Good morning! Welcome to Southeast Missouri. This time of year is often hard to figure out what to wear. One day it's in the 70s, the next day doesn't get out of the 40s. We wonder if we should wear long sleeves or shorts sleeves, and whether to wear multiple layers or maybe just a sweater or a jacket.

Before I leave my closet every day, I need to make sure that regardless of what clothes I decide to wear, that I also put on the full armor of God. In Ephesians 6:13–17, we are told what we need to wear to be "battle ready" for the day. Verse 13 says, "Therefore, take up the full armor of God, that you may be able to resist in the evil day, and having done everything, to stand firm." Then in verses 14-17, we are told what the full armor of God includes. We are told to wear the belt of truth, the breastplate of righteousness, to shod our feet with the preparation of the gospel of peace, the shield of faith, the helmet of salvation, and the sword of the Spirit, which is the word of God.

Jesus has already won the war, but to win the daily battles over the enemy, we need the help that we can only get from our Heavenly Father. Satan will do his best to shake us up during the day in order to get our focus off of God and onto our problems. But when we wear the full armor of God, the enemy will run into a brick wall, because we have what we need to stand firm. Wearing what God has provided for us, we can stand taller knowing that we will withstand today's battles. So, here's to being the victor that God intended us to be!

135...Sleep on It

Good morning! Have you ever given someone advice, only later needing to take it yourself? That happened to me a couple days ago. Several years ago, while teaching middle school, I noticed that emotions were running too much of their lives. So I gave them an acronym to use when those emotions came flooding over them … H. A. L. T. This acronym was to remind them to not make decisions when they were Hungry, Angry, Lonely, or Tired.

The hardest part about using this acronym is recognizing that one of those four things is going on in your life. As I mentioned, a few days ago I really needed this acronym, but just like my students, I had a hard time recognizing it. I had a really bad case of cabin fever. I was definitely hungry, lonely, and very tired from fighting this virus. I have to laugh about it now but then it was kind of serious. I was about ready to make a couple bad decisions. And then a girlfriend called and I was able to get wrapped up in the story she was telling me. When I got off the phone, I realized that none of the things I was thinking about doing made any sense at all.

The lonely part of the acronym was satisfied by her call, and after I went to the kitchen, the hungry part was also taken care of. Having a full belly, I was able to sleep and the next morning everything looked different. There's some real wisdom in "sleeping on it." When it comes to making wise decisions, we need to first turn to the Lord for His counsel. Proverbs 2:6 says, "For the Lord gives wisdom; from His mouth come knowledge and understanding." So when you find yourself out of sorts, and before you make ill-advised decisions, talk to the Lord about it. He might even bring the H.A.L.T. acronym to your mind. Here's to halting and yielding to His wisdom!

136...God Won

Good morning! There are many things that tell me Fall has arrived. The weather gets cooler, leaves start falling, the days get shorter, football season begins, and when you can walk out on your deck and walk straight into a spider web. Yikes!

I can easily wash that spider web off by taking a shower. But in life, there is one who tries his level best to entangle us in sin. Daily he tries to get us to ignore how God has instructed us to live. Reading in John 8:44, Jesus was talking about our enemy, Satan. "... he was a murderer from the beginning, and does not stand in the truth, because there's no truth in him. Whenever he speaks a lot, he speaks from his own nature; for he is a liar, and the father of lies."

Just like a football coach, Satan has a game plan. But once you learn his tactics, you can defeat him. He doesn't call any audibles, it's just the same old plan. He tells you his lies over and over, hoping one day that he can convince you of the lies. He wants you to believe things like you can never be good enough for God to love you (Lie #1), or that you've sinned too much to be forgiven (Lie #2).

Our good news and Satan's bad news can be found in James 4:7. "Submit therefore to God. Resist the devil and he will flee from you." We already know the final score of the enemy's game. It is and will continue to be ... God WON—Satan zero! My prayer for us today is that we would listen closely to the Holy Spirit as He steers us away from the enemy.

137...No Guarantees for Tomorrow

Good morning! Growing up I noticed that it wasn't always "what" you knew that got you places, but "who" you knew. That was particularly true when it came to finding jobs. You could have all the skills in the world but if you couldn't get your foot in the door, you would not be getting the opportunity that you were seeking. In our Christian life, we need to rely on both "what" we know and "who" we know. It's not enough to simply know that Jesus is the Son of God who sits at the right hand of His Father. We need to know that we are sinners and that we have a sin-debt that we could never pay. We need to know that Jesus died on the cross to satisfy that debt and because of that sacrifice, we can be covered by the Blood of Jesus. 2 Corinthians 5:21 says, "He made Him who knew no sin to be sin on our behalf, that we might become the righteousness of God in Him."

So that's the "what" of what we need but we also need the "who" to get our foot in Heaven. In order to be called one of God's children, we need a personal relationship with Jesus. John 10:27 says, "My sheep hear My voice, and I know them, and they follow Me; and I give eternal life to them, and they shall never perish; and no one shall snatch them out of My hand." Knowing that you could never satisfy God's requirement to be sin-free, have you asked Jesus to be your Lord and Savior? Until you do, Heaven will not be your eternal home. It's the "who" that provides what is needed for entrance. Just like we saw with those who passed away because of the October 2017 Las Vegas shootings, no one is guaranteed to-morrow. So, I'm praying you make the choice today, if you haven't already done so, to ask Jesus to be your Lord and Savior. It will be the best decision of your life!

138...Celebrate!

Good morning! Memories are such a sweet gift from God. They have a way of warming our hearts and reminding us of things that brought smiles to our faces. Memories can be recent or they can reach all the way back to when you were a child. I took a stroll down memory lane yesterday with my mother-in-law. Somehow we got talking about A&W Root Beer. When I was little, there used to be an A&W in the town I grew up in. My mom would take me there for special occasions or to celebrate a success, even if they were baby-step successes. Things like being able to correctly pronounce a new letter in my speech class or making progress with the physical therapy to straighten out my feet. When I get over this virus I'm fighting now, I'm looking forward to having a root beer float to celebrate being able to eat ice cream again!

As good as that celebration sounds in my head, there is no celebration on this earth that could hold a candle to the celebration in Heaven when someone here puts their trust in Jesus as their Lord and Savior. Luke 15:10 says it like this, "In the same way, I tell you, there is joy in the presence of the angels of God over one sinner who repents."

We can celebrate all kinds of things here on earth, but the one celebration we all need to have is when we give the angels a reason to sing praises as they celebrate us becoming a child of God. The decision is yours and Heaven is eagerly awaiting. So, here's to giving the angels of God something worth celebrating!

139...He's Right There

Good morning! There have been so many tragedies in 2017, and we still have two months left of this year. Hurricane Harvey, Irma, and Maria left behind destruction that will take years to recover from. Then there was the major earthquake in Mexico and the mass shooting in Las Vegas that will forever change the lives of many. So much heartache and loss. And now the fires out West are causing loss of lives and properties being burnt to the ground.

I heard someone say that "God must be asleep at the wheel." But nothing could be further from the truth! The earth that God created for us is described in Genesis 2:9-14. And then in verses 16 and 17, God gave the one restriction to this paradise He created for us. They were not to eat from the Tree of Knowledge of Good and Evil. We all know how this story ends. Adam and Eve ate from the forbidden tree, thus changing this world forever. Now before you say, "Thanks a lot, Adam," or "Thanks a lot, Eve," if it wasn't them who sinned, it could have very easily have been us. This is not how God created this world to be for us. The reason why we have these catastrophes going on is just a result of living in a fallen, sinful world.

God isn't asleep at the wheel. Look around at all the stories of people standing by and helping their neighbors, everyone coming together to rescue those in harm's way. And what about the stories being reported of organizations that rush in to the devastated areas to bring the basics of food, water, clothing and shelter. When you look at the good being done, there is where you will see God's hand at work. He is not asleep … He is in the middle of it all!

140...Working Out the Details

Good morning! Do you ever stop and look back at the journey that God has taken you on? Here's an example. Last week, I went to a new beautician because the lady that had been cutting my hair retired. I sent a text to a girlfriend from church who also does hair but she's wasn't taking new clients. Instead, she referred me to another lady in their salon. When I went there for my appointment, there was a young man sitting there talking to my new stylist. I wasn't there long before he asked me how I was doing. That caught me of guard because I didn't think I'd ever met this guy. Well, to make a very long story short, he was one of the First Responders that took care of me a few months ago when I got very sick and an ambulance was called. So as we talked about that, my stylist then told me she was also a First Responder. And as a matter of fact, because they live so close to me, if I ever needed assistance again, they would probably be the first ones on the scene. How cool is that??!!

God is in the details of our life. He has everything perfectly orchestrated so people that we need are put in our path at the perfect time. My encounter last week was just another example of that. Luke 12:7 says, "Indeed, the very hairs of your head are all numbered. Do not fear; you are of more value than any sparrows." My new beautician might not know the number of hairs on my head, but God sure does. That fact and the fact that I now know two of the people who could be here if I ever needed the help, brings me a lot of comfort. Thanking God this morning for showing me again that He's working out the details in my life and knowing He'll do the same thing for you! And may God bless the service of First Responders!

141...Let Love Rule Over Fear

Good morning! Think back to when you asked Jesus to be your Lord and Savior. What were your motivations behind asking Him to move into your heart? Was it about Him or was it mainly about you? For me, it was mainly about me. I accepted Jesus right before my first open-heart surgery in 1986. The doctors were not giving me good numbers as to whether this surgery would be successful. My decision to accept Jesus was out of my fear that if I should die, I wanted to be going to Heaven. Basically, I thought, "What do I have to lose?"

Over the years, I have discovered that most people come to their salvation decision out of fear for the consequences of their sinful lives. But the cool thing is that God knows our motivation and accepts us into His family anyway. Luke 23:39-43 gives us the account of the two criminals that were also being crucified with Jesus. One man hurled insults at Jesus but the other man repented and asked Jesus to remember him when He entered Heaven. And in verse 43 Jesus says to this man, "Truly I say to you, today you shall be with Me in Paradise." Out of fear this man turned to Jesus as he was dying, and Jesus accepted him.

The difference between this criminal and us is that he had no time to know and serve Jesus because his life on earth was soon to be over. But for us, hopefully, we can make that decision to accept Jesus as our Lord and Savior and still have time to learn more about Him and serve Him until our life ends here on earth. So today, I am thankful that the Lord took my decision, based on a selfish motivation, and has allowed me to learn how to obediently follow Him out of love and devotion, instead of fear. Praying you've made the same decision.

142...PATIENTLY WAITING

Good morning! A girlfriend sent me a picture that made me laugh and also shake my head in agreement. It was a picture of a dog sitting on a porch watching something eat his food. The caption read, "Two of the greatest qualities to have in life are ... patience and wisdom."

Waiting is not my strong suit. Can you relate? Over the years though, I have discovered that there's a lot of wisdom in patiently waiting on the Lord. Psalm 27:14 tells us to, "Wait for the Lord; be strong, and let your heart take courage; yes, wait for the Lord." I know I need to be more like the farmer in James 5:7-8. "Be patient, therefore, brethren, until the coming of the Lord. Behold, the farmer waits for the precious produce of the soil, being patient about it, until it gets the early and late rains. You too be patient; strengthen your hearts, for the coming of the Lord is at hand."

These verses tell us that we have a job to do as we wait on the Lord. We are to be strong, courageous, and that we should strengthen our hearts. The best way I've found to satisfy those things that we're to do is to get knee deep in God's Word. His Word is where you'll find the strength to be courageous and the power to strengthen your heart. It definitely pays off to wait on the Lord. When we don't, things typically don't turn out well. Oh, by the way, on the picture that my girlfriend sent me, the thing eating the dog's food, was a skunk! LOL ☺ So, here's to exercising the wisdom of waiting patiently on the Lord.

142

143...Having it All

Good morning! Time is one of those things that we can't seem to get enough of. I was thinking about time as this weekend we will be "falling back" due to Daylight Savings Time ending. Even though this time change will affect what time it is when it gets dark, there is literally nothing we can do to add even one minute to our days.

Our life comes down to how we spend the twenty-four hours that God gives us each day. Are we spending our time glorifying God or ourselves? Romans 12:14 tells us that one day, when we stand before the throne of God, we will have to give God an account of the time He gave us here on earth. Are you ready to answer to how you have spent your time? I don't think any of us are, but the good news is that we can change that fact starting right now.

So then, how does God want us to spend our days? I think what Jesus had to say in Matthew 28:19 answers that question for us. "Go therefore and make disciples of all the nations, baptizing them in the name of the Father and the Son and the Holy Spirit teaching them to observe all I commanded you ..."

We have been placed here on earth to glorify God and to share the Good News of Jesus. We live in a world that desperately needs to hear about Jesus so others can understand the freedom that comes from giving our life over to the Lord. We need to pass on the same hope in the Lord that we've experienced as Believers, because if we have hope in Jesus, we have it all.

144...Getting What We Don't Deserve

Good morning! Living out life is like a gymnast doing a routine on a balance beam. Sometimes we pull off a nearly perfect performance, and other times, we fall off the beam and land on the mat. That's one thing that I absolutely love about God ... when we fall, He gives us a mat to land on!

It's all about His immeasurable grace and inexhaustible mercy. God's grace is when He gives us what we don't deserve, like a mat to soften our fall. His grace gives us the good things in life when we absolutely don't deserve anything good because of our sinful ways. Along with God's grace, He lavishly covers us with His mercy. This is when God doesn't give us what we do deserve because of our sins. We don't deserve a soft landing when we fall. Because of our sinful lives, we deserve to land face down on a hard, concrete floor.

Hebrews 4:15-16 says,

> For we do not have a High Priest who cannot sympathize with our weaknesses, but one who has been tempted in all things as we are, yet without sin. Let us therefore draw near with confidence to the throne of grace, that we may receive mercy and may find grace to help in time of need.

God understands what we go through in the course of our days. Temptations are all around us and sometimes we fall off the beam, but God is right there ready to offer us His mercy. He helps us recognize our error and then gets us back up on the beam, and then we try again. So, here's to worshiping God, that through His incredible love for His children, gives us a mat to land on!

145...FLIP SIDE OF THE COIN

Good morning! During this month of Thanksgiving, we focus on the blessings we've received and spend time thanking God for all of them. But could I challenge us to look at this month in another way? I'm finding that there is a flip side to the "thank you God for …" coin.

The other side of that coin says, "Thank you God that I am able to …" We've all heard the phrase, "It's better to give than receive." The giving side of the coin is something that would benefit us to take a closer look at. When is the last time you sat down and spent some time thinking about what kind of blessings you could pass on to others? Giving to others makes you an extension of God's love, which is pretty cool.

I'm not talking about humongous things, like buying someone a house, but the little things that could definitely make someone's day. An example of the simpler things that have made my day is when someone sends me a card just to say hi and to let me know they're thinking about me. Don't you just love getting mail when it's something other than bills???

In the book of Colossians, Paul was explaining how Believers should change into the way God has already made them by His saving grace. Their new lives in Christ should reflect the Lord and others should see that their old ways have been replaced with a Godly love for one another. Colossians 3:14 says, "And beyond all these things put on love, which is the perfect bond of unity." So then, there is a question we need to answer. How can we bless others as an extension of the blessings God has poured out on us? It's a question worth answering.

146...Life Worth Living

Good morning! Can you believe how fast time goes by? It seems like I was just starting this devotional but I am now actually writing the next to the last entry. This has definitely been a new chapter in my life. New chapters usually happen when something big rocks our world. Some of the new chapters are inspired by something wonderful in life, like the arrival of a new baby, and some are forced on you, like when you experience the loss of someone you love. For me, writing these devotionals started with the loss of Alan and they continue because Alan and I want to make sure our future generations can share in our faith.

Regardless of the reason, I see new beginnings as ways for God to once again show Himself mightily in our lives. And that's what God does best! But what's our part in these new beginnings? I like how Paul wrote about this in Colossians 1:10. Paul was writing about the reason why they were praying for the Colossians' growth. "... so that you may walk in a manner worthy of the Lord, to please Him in all respects, bearing fruit in every good work and increasing in the knowledge of God ..."

There are many things we can strive for in each new chapter of our lives, but I think that if at the end of the journey, we can say that we spent our time learning and carrying out what pleases God, we could claim that we were successful. No, it's not the same way the "world" defines success, but the benefits of doing it God's way far outweigh the benefits that the world offers. So, here's to doing our best to live a life worthy of the Lord!

147...Much More than a Reminder

Good morning! Have you ever noticed that our feelings and reality are not always the same? Sometimes when we are in the middle of a situation, we don't recognize that difference. I've been talking to the Lord a lot lately about how quiet and lonely many of my nights are without Alan being here. The loneliness is the way I feel, but it's not reality.

Deuteronomy 31:6 gives me what the reality of my situation actually is. "Be strong and courageous, do not be afraid or tremble at them, for the Lord your God is the one who goes with you. He will not fail you or forsake you." The Lord is always with me. I just forget that sometimes, so our gracious and compassionate Lord has given me a reminder. We have a grandfather clock sitting on the fireplace mantle. Alan would wind this "7-day" clock every Sunday morning. With Alan passing away on a Sunday, it hasn't been touched since his death, which is over a year now.

A couple of days ago, as I was talking to my sister on the phone, the pendulum started swinging on the clock and then the chimes went off. At first it kind of freaked me out and then I realized what was happening. God is so sweet! The clock chimes on the hour and the half hour and those 48 times a day that the clock now chimes are my 48 reminders from God that I'm not alone. The next day, I went to see the man who has worked on the clock before to learn how to wind it correctly. A couple of days later I told this story to Alan's son. He asked me what time the clock had stopped on. It knew it was 1:20 because the minute hand was over the hole that one of the keys needed to go in to wind it and the gentleman I talked to about how to wind the clock told me it was OK to move the minute hand out of the way. Still not making the connection, he asked me what time Alan died. He passed away at 1:20. All this time the clock was sitting on 1:20 and I never even noticed it's significance. So now every Sunday, I will wind the clock and thank God for the reminders He is giving me every thirty minutes that I am not alone. And if I am not alone, how can I be lonely?

God wants to do more than remind you that you're never alone. He wants to offer

you the gift of salvation. We can all agree that life has its ups and downs. With these challenges, we can either go with God's flow and allow Him to navigate the streams in our lives, or we can fight the current and try to do things on our own. Swimming against the current is not only hard to do, it doesn't get us very far. The solution to living life where we don't have to swim upstream is Jesus. If you haven't yet experienced the hope of Jesus, there is no better day than today to ask Him to be your Lord and Savior and allow Him to guide your days, no matter what waterways you find yourself in. I pray you make that decision so that one day, when we are all in Heaven, I can introduce you to Alan. May God bless you!

Linda Estes has mastered the
one minute devotional!

Henry Neufeld
Owner
Energion Publications

"My choice was reduced, then, not to
whether I'd be a caregiver, but more
what kind of caregiver I'd be."

– **Robert Martin**

MORE FROM ENERGION PUBLICATIONS

Personal Study

Finding My Way in Christianity	Herold Weiss	$16.99
The Jesus Paradigm	David Alan Black	$17.99
When People Speak for God	Henry Neufeld	$17.99

Christian Living

Faith in the Public Square	Robert D. Cornwall	$16.99
Grief: Finding the Candle of Light	Jody Neufeld	$8.99
Directed Paths	Myrtle Neufeld	$9.99
Pathways to Prayer	David Moffett-Moore	$5.99

Bible Study

Learning and Living Scripture	Lentz/Neufeld	$12.99
Luke: A Participatory Study Guide	Geoffrey Lentz	$8.99
Philippians: A Participatory Study Guide	Bruce Epperly	$9.99
Ephesians: A Participatory Study Guide	Robert D. Cornwall	$9.99
Meditations on According to John	Herold Weiss	$14.99
The Jesus Manifesto	David Moffett-Moore	$9.99
Those Footnotes in Your Bible	Thomas W. Hudgins	$5.99

Theology

Creation in Scripture	Herold Weiss	$12.99
Creation: the Christian Doctrine	Edward W. H. Vick	$12.99
Ultimate Allegiance	Robert D. Cornwall	$9.99
The Journey to the Undiscovered Country	William Powell Tuck	$9.99
From Here to Eternity	Bruce Epperly	$5.99

Ministry

Clergy Table Talk	Kent Ira Groff	$9.99
So Much Older Then …	Robert LaRochelle	$9.99
Wind and Whirlwind	David Moffett-Moore	$9.99
A Positive Word for Christian Lamenting	William Powell Tuck	$16.99

Generous Quantity Discounts Available
Dealer Inquiries Welcome
Energion Publications — P.O. Box 841
Gonzalez, FL 32560
Website: http://energionpubs.com
Phone: (850) 525-3916

CPSIA information can be obtained
at www.ICGtesting.com
Printed in the USA
FFOW04n0449190218
45072526-45454FF